PRAC
IMPACTFUL HUMAN RESOURCES FOR SMEs

For CEOs and HR leaders who do not want to become a failed SME statistic

RICHARD COWLEY

PASSIONPRENEUR®
P U B L I S H I N G

Publishing information
Publishing, design, and production facilitated by Passionpreneur Publishing
www.PassionpreneurPublishing.com

Content developed using the support of the Ultimate 48 Hour Author
www.48HourAuthor.me

Tel: 1 300 664 006
Diamond Creek
Melbourne, Victoria
Australia 3089

*I dedicate this book to Lotte and Ryan,
my darling children who help me be a better person
and father every moment of every day.*

*To May and John, my mother and father, who have always
been themselves and done their best to inspire me.
Sadly, 2020 was their last year on this planet and it is
with deep sadness that I acknowledge that they will
never read this book. Their passing inspired me to be
brave, publish this book and live a YOLO life.*

*To my brother John Jnr, who has taught me the
importance of integrity, my sister Theresa who has been
the mainstay of our family.*

*To my partner Yu, who brings daily happiness and a
sense of humbleness to my life.*

To the great leaders I have had the pleasure to work with over the years: Nick and Paul @ Royal Navy, John @ British Aerospace, Phil and David @ DHL, John and Bob @ Coca-Cola, Tom, Ken, Jem, Kristy, Kylie, Phyllis @ Kimberly-Clark, Bent, Dag, Andrew, Peter and Per @ Tetra Pak. Sanil, my dearest friend and confidant, and partner in all things IT, and Greg and Rik, the best business advisors and friends.

To my true friends, you know who you are, all of who have inspired me and been there through the high and lows of my corporate and personal life.

The theme of all the people above is that they inspired, motivated, taught me, led me, grew me, cried with me, laughed with me, and ultimately cared about me. They taught me to keep going and believe in myself and keep contributing until the fear inside went away.

TABLE OF CONTENTS

TESTIMONIALS

Richard is an expert within all disciplines in human resource development. He is very international-focused, with extensive experience in the Middle East and Asia. He is capable of being a driver in change management in order to step-change organisations to be more competitive. He is a top-notch recruiter who cut to the bone to find the best possible candidates for senior executive positions.

—Bo Lundberg, CEO, General Manager and Board Member, Denmark & Saudi Arabia

With an incredible affinity for people and possessing incredible passion and energy, Richard is one of those rare team members who delivers not only the project but the enthusiasm and goodwill of the broader organisation. A leader in the HR arena, Richard showed his versatility and capability by successfully delivering critical projects across our regional sales program.

—David Osborn, Director and CEO

Richard is an outstanding Human Resource professional. He has deep insight into organisational and talent development requirements for businesses to be successful in today's highly competitive markets. He is an exceptional talent identifier, a tremendously passionate and forthright colleague who inspires every single person that he meets. He combines superb topic expertise with a high level of personal integrity, energy, and creativity that most can't match. I have worked with HR professionals across many markets over a long career and Richard is at the top of my list.

**—Ken Whitaker, Global Business Leader,
excellence in brand growth and P&L management**

I have engaged Richard on two occasions and highly recommend him for his change management capabilities, drive, action orientation, and business acumen. Richard led an organisational transformation program to support me in the regionalisation of our technical service organisation comprising 600+ employees across Asia. He delivered excellent results through his ability to balance results and people orientation. His ability to apply his deep HR expertise with an understanding of business realities is outstanding, and he has had a profound impact on the Asia organisation. On the second occasion, he stepped into a temporary role as a HR business partner and again demonstrated the tenacity and action orientation that we needed as well as drawing on his HR knowledge.

**—Peter Mott, Professor of Practice,
Engineering Business Management at University of Bath**

Richard has provided a personal development course which over half of our Asia-wide staff have attended. The feedback is very positive, and I believe the results are starting to show. If you want to make a "step-change" in your organisation, consider talking to Richard.

—Andrew Pooch, Managing Director

Richard is one of the most talented, if not the most talented, HR person I have known and had the pleasure to work with in my thirty-year-plus career. He brings an uncanny insight to any situation as well as a very strong business acumen. KCC truly misses Richard.

—Tim Baade, Senior Vice President and General Manager

Richard worked with me as HR Director. In this role, he was focused on improving the way we build global capabilities aligned with our long-term business strategy. He did a great job of driving multiple projects focused on building strategic capabilities in the organisation. He is able to combine his deep HR expertise with a strong business understanding in order to partner with the line organisation. Richard holds very high standards for himself and is also able to establish this for the teams that he manages. I've known Richard to be exceptional at bringing new ideas to light when others continue to offer more in-line solutions or ideas. He is a personable, passionate individual who is valued by his colleagues for her insightful advice and positive perspective. I recommend Richard for larger and more complex business partner roles in any industry.

—John Argabright, Vice President of human resources

Richard is an insightful leader, which sets him apart. He has an outstanding ability to translate complex challenges into impactful solutions and outcomes in a way that inspires the very best of a team and makes the most of the biggest opportunities. I have had the privilege to work with Richard across several businesses for over twenty years. Turning around an underperforming $US100 million operation might sound daunting but it seemed like a breeze to Richard. He brings purpose, focus, order and structure while fostering ambition, achievement, camaraderie, and enjoyment. For any company or team seeking to optimise performance, Richards is your guy. His get-things-done-with-a-smile approach is infectious and galvanising.

—David Atkinson, Managing Director, DHL

I have worked together with Richard on several projects, projects that have spanned over large regional areas (South East Asia, Oceania and North Asia) as well as a higher number of employees (600+). Richard has brought HR knowledge, professionalism and experience to these projects in combination with extremely structured project management skills. What differentiates him from most people I have worked with, is his passion and drive, both for the task at hand, as well as all the people involved. The passion for people and how they contribute is the base for everything Richard does. Richard also has a great ability when it comes to finding the right way forward. He does so by challenging you and asking the right questions to drive conclusions and alignment. A true professional that I will bring to any organisational and people-related projects in the future.

—Bent Olufsen, Global Account Director Services, Tetra Pak

AUTHOR BIO

**I partner with leaders to deliver business
opportunities and create value.**

**I am passionate about helping teams and
individuals achieve.**

**I am committed to helping economies grow through
grassroots contribution.**

As a globally experienced HR leader, I have spent most of my illustrious thirty-eight-year HR career delivering the organisational aspirations of large global MNC companies including military, aerospace, fast-moving consumer goods, automation machines, logistics, and supply chain. These have included the Royal Navy, British Aerospace, DHL, Coca-Cola, Kimberly-Clark, and Tetra Pak. By contrast, my SME experience exposure has been in the food, health and beverage, office equipment, construction, machine and automation, cycling, jewellery, multi-level marketing personal care, AI HR software, recruitment and outsourcing; information technology and software founder of my own heavily invested HR technology start up.

I have been responsible for providing HR functional leadership and transactional support for over 20,000 employees of all levels and job types in country, regional, and global roles covering more than twenty-five countries.

I have developed, led and facilitated over forty global, regional, national or functional transformation change programs in various project, leadership and workforce contexts.

I have led over fifty business-focused OGSM business strategy and performance alignment, coaching and feedback sessions.

I have been a recruitment specialist at all levels of recruitment as well as a LinkedIn recruiter. I was hired in developing and emerging markets including Asia, the Middle East, North Africa, Oceania, the USA, and the UK.

I have led and been a team member in the development of global/local human resource system platforms and later in my career started my own HR technology company to deliver a truly exceptional recruitment platform, raising over 2 million dollars.

My key capabilities and passions are business opportunity delivery, organisational capability development, digital application and transformation (machine learning, data science, natural language programming, chatbot, SaaS), talent and performance management, and very hands-on delivery. I am very passionate about helping people, technology and process innovation, and making a social impact.

I believe that the HR function has significantly more to contribute to the delivery of business objectives and works with HR practitioners and leaders to make this a reality. My focus is on five areas:

1. The future economy, so future generations have opportunities and workplace fulfilment.
2. Sustainable delivery of organisational business opportunities that in turn drive economic growth.
3. Equip leaders with technology-enabled tools required to drive high team performance, and ultimately, business objectives.
4. Help individuals take control of their career journey to achieve their aspirations.
5. Enhance human resources contributions in the workplace – move from the perception of a support function to that of an effective business enabler.

I founded www.onehr.world because I was fuelled by a desire to help people achieve in the workplace, and had an unwavering belief in the untapped potential of HR to power organisational objectives. My mission is to bring this philosophy to life by helping people achieve.

I am a firm believer in the power of conversation to drive actionable change and would be happy to share insights and ideas, and brainstorm all things HR.

In summary, I have three core passions my daughter Charlotte, who is on her way to becoming a talented play therapist, and my son Ryan, who is a talented lighting designer, and all things HR.

I love windsurfing, fitness, diving, cooking, rugby, chess, football and working!

Full Name: Richard Andrew Ian Cowley
Alias: Richard HR Cowley
Skype: Richard Andrew Ian Cowley
Email: rich.c@onehr.world
Platform: www.onehr.world
LinkedIn: https://www.linkedin.com/in/cowleyrich/
WhatsApp: +66818758590
Facetime: +66818758590

1

POTENTIAL REASONS
FOR FAILURE

Most small and medium-sized enterprises (SMEs) allegedly fail for four main reasons: inexperience of the business owner; no business or action plan; no capital/funding; or a bad idea. However, the reality is that there are many other reasons that we can manage and thus ensure we do not become a failed SME!

> "Your time is limited, so don't waste it living someone else's life."
>
> — Steve Jobs

There are many wonderful reasons that a founder or owner starts their own business, and it is generally not by choice that they have to close their business because of failure or non-achievement of their aspiration.

If we can accept the reality that SMEs generally fail because of these four main reasons and many others, then it is not an overstatement to say that taking proactive and assertive action to minimise their potential impact can ensure our SME does not become one of these 'failed' statistics. This practice is not complicated but will demand an open mind, discipline, beliefs, and behaviour generally contrary to those of an entrepreneur, founder, owner, and HR team. A critical partnership can truly enable the success, growth, and achievement of a sustainable business. Without this, team members are doomed to ponder what could have been!

Been there, done that (got the t-shirt)!

I wear my SME HR technology start-up failure as a badge of honour because I followed my dream, my heart, and my passions, and I did not settle for 'thinking about it' even though I was in a very comfortable corporate HR world with opportunities before me. I see my career journey as the greatest accelerated personal development experience one can have. In failure, I have learned and grown. Even the pain, reflections and disappointment I must have caused my investors – most of whom were friends – continues to impact me. However, I have turned these negative feelings into an altruistic purpose – to share and help other SME organisations so that they do not experience the same missed opportunities, negatively impacted relationships and financial setbacks. I continue to believe that by helping individuals, teams and organisations, we can help economies sustainably grow. I specifically believe that by helping SME HR leaders in many different ways to deliver a winning partnership with their SME leadership team, we will achieve a reduction in SME failures; it is possible and we can do it together.

Where there's a will there's a way!

A simple proverb that has defined my life: my determination has helped me overcome many obstacles and accomplish so much, both professionally and personally, and it can for you too.

My journey as a HR practitioner and partner began in the Royal Navy in the personnel department. From there, my career took me around the world, employed by some of the largest and well-known brand names on the planet with huge HR budgets to some of the smallest and unknown brands in their country, where investment in HR is generally the last thought and yet often the most required.

With no secondary school qualifications, dyslexia, poor English vocabulary and spelling ability, low confidence, self-esteem, and frankly no strategic HR education, I transformed my career by being able to overcome any adversity. My drive and action orientation mean I complete what I start, and my obsession for achievement and helping others enabled me to build credibility and belief. This is complemented by my passion for life, innovation, and creativity. I have an appetite for learning which has been a constant in my life through formal knowledge and application. I also possess an innate ability and deep-rooted delight in connecting and helping others, but the icing on the cake is my zeal for diligence and hard work.

All the above enabled me to accomplish so much including a successful global corporate HR career where I have delivered in all the roles of HR in some capacity. I have worked on most continents of the world in country, regional, project or global roles. The context has also varied including the military, engineering, logistics, fast-moving consumer goods, automation machinery, information and HR technology to superfood industries, working alongside entrepreneurs, founders, leaders, and employees from all functions. My journey has taken me through a HR career path of generalist and specialist roles to being a HR entrepreneur myself to a passion and recent focus on business partnering, transformation and change, or simply put, delivering the business aspiration.

By contrast, my SME experience is where I have had some of my most challenging moments and most significant 'aha' experiences. My SME company exposure includes my early experiences in UK fish and chip and hamburger fast food outlets, office equipment, and huge learning at my parents' pub.

In the last decade, I have supported a UK construction building group, a French machine manufacturer, a US fibreglass bicycle manufacturer, Thailand jewellery OEM, a New Zealand multi-level marketing personal care, a Saudi Arabian food brand, and an Indian HR artificial intelligence technology, a Swedish and global specialist recruitment, a Thailand spirulina superfood, my own Luxembourg/Hong Kong/India/Sri Lanka/Thailand HR technology start-up and now a Thailand information technology business.

All enterprises have been different in terms of size, scope, home base, industry, stage of evolution, funds and, most importantly, business aspiration and leadership. I have drawn upon my many large enterprise global experiences whilst concurrently adapting and developing new ways of working to ensure I could be as successful in an SME as in a large enterprise. It has demanded that I continually evaluate the business landscape, organisation aspirations and ways of working and then adapt all that I know and have applied to ensure applicability, ensuring what I am going to do or recommend is practical and helpful versus putting further strain and demand on leaders and colleagues who are already overwhelmed or challenged by their context.

Same same but different!

While seemingly similar, each SME organisation has been different in so many ways, some of the obvious being the varying industries, customers, products or services, job types, cash flow, process orientation, technology sophistication, stage of growth and scaling up. The more complex and profound were the founders/owners/leaders' backgrounds, ways of working, tolerance for ambiguity, business and financial acumen, personalities and most importantly to me, their leadership style. From a HR perspective, there are also significant differences depending on the HR leader and the financial situation and stage of development of the SME.

Fundamentally, even with all of these differences, there have been some absolute similarities that are globally consistent for any SME. As is generally the case, there are benefits, pros and cons, opportunities or challenges as we like to semantically express in HR.

SME challenges I have faced

I could spend many hours sharing all the positive experiences I have encountered being employed in SME organisations, however, this book is about the challenges I faced as a HR Leader supporting SMEs and how to address them. I listened to many candidates talk about their experiences working for an SME during the hiring process before I actually started to be employed by them myself—my own experiences have only reinforced their beliefs. This list is probably global, as there are consistent themes in what I consider to be a non-prioritised list. The weighting of each really is driven by the context of the organisation with some being more relevant for some and potentially all of them being relevant for all at some point. I recommend you tick the ones that are relevant to you in your organisation's leadership or HR role to provide insights and awareness.

The founder/owner/CEO/MD background – whatever term we want to use – is the starting point and the most senior representative of the company. Past predicts the future – SMEs are generally led by six categories of people, based on the principle that the past predicts the future. It is their background that often leads to the success or failure of an SME:

- ☐ **Entrepreneurs** who have little education and/or business exposure who had an idea or a passion to go it alone.
- ☐ **Seasoned large enterprise business professionals** with pristine education and demonstrated successful experience in leading and growing businesses who had a passion to try to build their own company.
- ☐ **Professionals with particular knowledge and experience** that they believe they can leverage or develop by offering a new product, service or solution to the world.
- ☐ **Professionals who want to put a start-up on their CV,** believing that it would be a great experience and/or lead to greater freedom and potentially if all goes to plan, a huge financial upside.

- ☐ **Accidental SME leaders** who did not intentionally set off down the path of becoming a SME owner/founder/leader but through some twist of fate or context became one.
- ☐ **Serial SME leaders** who have demonstrated experience in starting, growing and potentially selling an SME organisation.

In all six examples above, there are reasons to believe the leader could/could not lead an SME to success, what is clear is that if you are doing it for the first time, as is often the case, you have much to learn and require support, new knowledge and education to accelerate your journey, reduce risks and maximise the chance of success.

- ☐ **Their way or the highway** – A common phrase indicating that this leadership group has their own ways of working and thinking, often not seeking input or feedback or appearing to be open but actually placating or suppressing others' feelings.
- ☐ **Comfort zones** – Very rarely does this group possess all the technical and personal competencies. As such, they tend to lead within their comfort zone. This can culminate in a focus on the areas they are most knowledgeable or comfortable versus what is most critical and important to the organisation's aspiration.
- ☐ **Taking things personally or making things personal** – I believe it is a common trait among people but if it's your company, you can't help but have a sense of ownership. This means you will find it hard to accept criticism or negative

feedback even when the intent is positive, which it often is. How this manifests itself is the signal to the team and builds beliefs as to whether they are employed in a working environment where contributions are welcome, need to be delivered sensitively or can be expressed freely. It is less about the organisation and personalities, differences are highlighted through making things about me and you, i.e., personal versus professional.

☐ **Not invented here** – Not sure of the reason, however, as the 'boss' there is a real sense that all ideas need to come from the top or be seen as such, building an 'I know the best' belief. You may see shared ideas from the team 'reappear' a few weeks or months later with the boss as the instigator, or a variation on the theme.

☐ **Leadership definition** – Often first and last to speak, believing it is their role (or right) to lead the team through all discussions. In the same way, their belief means they will lead with a more authoritarian top-down approach. Recognising of course that this confidence and belief is often the reason they are 'different' and lead a company versus being employed. Making all the final decisions, and controlling as much as possible is a belief held which reduces organisational speed, and freedom to act and reinforces conservatism and greater political behaviour.

☐ **It's my company, my team, my family, my employees** – Yes indeed and as a former owner/founder I can confirm that you live in a bubble where you truly believe you have the ultimate responsibility and this can lead to individual approaches to many situations based on these beliefs, whether it be the way forward for the company to individual people decisions.

☐ **Mini-me** – If everyone was like me then our company would grow. Hiring, decision-making, and developing team members based on a high belief about themselves leads to a cloning exercise where everyone at the party is the same. As we all know, we think in many different ways, e.g., learning styles and thought processes, and we can't expect the same from all. This understanding appears void at times.

☐ **Work ethic** – Expectations are high in an SME, with work ethic often being questioned and owners working long hours and expecting the same from the team, however, forgetting that the greater reward of their stock price, profits or company value will benefit them not the team unless shares or profit share have been communicated.

☐ **Walk the talk** – A much-discussed area, 'do as I say not as I do' leads to a contradiction, which ultimately leaves people confused. This can manifest itself in so many ways e.g., expressing 'we need to be innovative and creative' and yet pushing back on ideas that don't fit with their comfort zones, to spending on new cars and other items but not rewarding employees with a bonus or annual increments.

☐ **Favourites and cliques** – We all have them, however, in SME organisations this tendency to make decisions based on having favourites or being members of established cliques can lead to an exaggerated culture of needing to stand out, becoming more political or expressing only complementary thinking or expressions, i.e., sucking up. Newbies can find this incredibly challenging as they try to navigate these established groups that do not make it easy for anyone wanting to make a change or integrate. This is almost unconscious discrimination.

☐ **Unethical or illegal practices** – Impact or are contrary to employee beliefs or a sense of fair play.

☐ **The tendency to act with the end in mind without clarity and focus** – It is imperative to think long term with the end in mind. The challenge comes when this requires translation into action now. How to prioritise and focus the organisation's resources in terms of time, cash flow and people is not a nice problem to have, it's an imperative. Generally, I have seen (sometimes) a complete lack of detailed connection between daily actions and the long-term plan with the belief that the broad aspiration and goal are sufficient to guide the necessary objectives and actions. We call it business planning in large companies and is typically an annual event with periodic, monthly or quarterly dialogue to track and take action to ensure adherence to the plan.

☐ **Mindreading** – A skill we can't possess, however, I have seen too many times an environment where the team, at all levels, is expected to understand the organisation's way forward and to connect this to their decision-making and their role.

☐ **Getting ahead of ourselves or getting carried away** – Often with limited resources and cash flow or indeed overwhelmed by investment with more resources and cash flow than we have managed before, we get a false sense of security. This leads to decisions that are not in the best interests of the company. There are too many examples here but let me share a few important ones: opening many finance entities believing this will make us feel and look like a global company before we have sold anything; renting (fixed cost) or buying assets that are not sustainable or ahead of their need or not required; setting up complex or overmanaged processes; hiring too many people or the wrong people; increasing fixed costs when there are other solutions; building products or solutions that are beyond the market need or are unproven.

☐ **Organisation capability investment** – What you don't know you don't know – not many SME leaders have led, in any capacity, a total organisation towards a business aspiration. To compound these fundamental gaps in strategic know-how and knowledge, how many have had the experience or education of building the future capability of an organisation to meet the potentially ever-changing and often complex context?

☐ **SME Education** – There are very few business degrees or general management education programs that provide both the principles and the model, templates, and tools to help build an SME plan. SME leaders of strategy, process and people are often not continually developed as they take on new accountabilities and responsibilities that they are not prepared or educated sufficiently to manage, an almost sink or swim mentality is adopted, hoping they will be successful.

☐ **Organisational investment** – There is a lack of focus on organisational investment, structure, people development and short-mid-term planning – cash flow is king, however, sustainable growth and scaling up will be enabled by the 'right' level of investment in future capability.

☐ **Dynamic and deliberate versus fixed and evolving strategy** – Yes, it is exhausting at times, both physically and mentally, working in an SME. Given this deep thinking, organisational development in addition to business planning meetings may feel like overkill, not required, or necessary only once a year. My experience is that given the nature of SMEs, they need more investment of time in this area than large enterprises as their environment is very dynamic and resources are tight so being deliberate in planning will ensure minimum waste and high productivity. Discipline to review periodically, e.g., monthly will ensure no gaps appear; it should never be considered set in stone.

☐ **Organisational clarity is going to help** – Size does not negate a need for structure driven by strategy, job clarity, and clear role accountabilities. Often expressed that we are so small people don't need to consider the structure, employees don't need detailed job descriptions, or we need everyone to contribute in many areas so leaving it open is best. This thinking will lead to role overlap, accountability confusion and most importantly (and I've seen it so many times), employees will be left to their own devices, to do what they are good at, enjoy doing or think is important. It simply is unproductive and leads to waste on a number of levels.

Next we move to the current start-up fad, en vogue – increased number of employees applying to start-up SMEs, with huge prevailing beliefs compounded by the growth of SMEs to mega global organisations.

☐ **Freedom to act – A major perceived upside to working for a start-up is the freedom to contribute strategically** and to think/act with fewer constraints than a large organisation. The reality is that the founder/owner/senior leader often has their own boundaries and these can be less transparent than in large organisations.

☐ **The grass is not greener** – The stated and much-acclaimed personal benefits of SME employment like flexible working hours with a focus on work-life balance, e.g., picking up kids and a more casual working culture are over-stated by the reality of a greater reliance on your contribution and critical deadlines. It is not unheard of for many SME employees to be working weekends and evenings with pressure or coercion being subtly applied.

☐ **Outcome misalignment** – Yes, we have all seen the various but minimal successes of some SMEs that have exponential stock growth and get-in early benefits for employees including stock options. The reality is that only a few reap the reward of this perceived benefit, it truly is a fallacy that is fast becoming transparent and recognised.

☐ **Employment stability** – One of the major things that I hear and see a lot is the perceived need for employment stability, especially in these uncertain times. It appears doable in the first instance, however, when you join an SME and live with the constant potential belief that you might not be paid on time if at all, long-term employment is not guaranteed and the worst case is your savings plan (if you have one) or severance is not paid and thus this employment time does not add value to your career.

Human resources related areas is our last significant topic to share and is illustrative of the major SME challenges I have encountered:

☐ **Leadership style** – Large enterprise organisations are generally led foremost by seasoned business professionals with pristine education and demonstrated successful experience in leading and growing businesses and people. Adept at working within a structure, process and cultural norms. SMEs by contrast are generally led by passionate, driven, independent, and confident individuals who I consider 'brave'. The culture can be unstructured, highly dynamic, and driven by the founder/owner's personal preferences and beliefs versus what is best for the organisation. Both have their pros/cons, of course, for SMEs this somewhat maverick personality carries with it specific beliefs and behaviours that will generally challenge leaders or employees who make the transition from large enterprise organisations. The experience is invaluable, however, this can manifest itself in frustration as the opportunity to contribute fully can be limited. For leaders who have been employed in SMEs all their careers, these limitations are known and accepted and appear to have suppressed their will to challenge, contribute, and change.

☐ **HR accountability confusion and prioritisation** – from a HR responsibility perspective, there can be up to twenty-six core accountabilities (see later chapter) that a HR Leader is responsible for leading/managing in a large organisation. These need to be adapted depending on the SME context. These can be categorised under four main areas of responsibility:

1. HR business partner (HRBP)
2. HR functional partner (HRFP)
3. HR governance and performance (HRG&PE)
4. HR innovation and development (HRI&D)

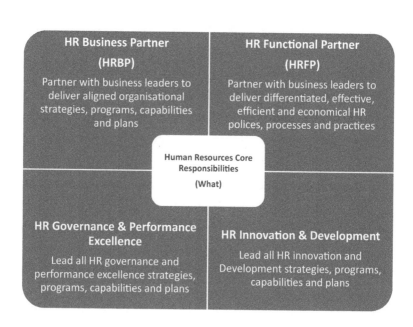

HR Business Partner (HRBP)
Partner with business leaders to deliver aligned organisational strategies, programs, capabilities and plans

HR Functional Partner (HRFP)
Partner with business leaders to deliver differentiated, effective, efficient and economical HR polices, processes and practices

Human Resources Core Responsibilities (What)

HR Governance & Performance Excellence
Lead all HR governance and performance excellence strategies, programs, capabilities and plans

HR Innovation & Development
Lead all HR innovation and Development strategies, programs, capabilities and plans

☐ **Too much admin focus** – By contrast, depending on their context, SMEs may require all twenty-six core accountabilities at a specific time, however, they generally focus delivery on personnel accountabilities, as we used to call them. For instance, HR policy and administration, recruitment, performance management, employee relations and compliance with labour law, with learning and development potentially having a role as organisations become medium-size.

☐ **Hiring inappropriate HR talent** – Given the above context, depending on their stage of evolution and size, SMEs hire the following HR profiles:

- HR administrators who have the potential to deliver the immediate administration-related requirements.
- Personnel managers or officers who may have the potential to grow or contribute at a higher level as the SME scales up and grows.
- HR managers who are generalists with similar SME experiences.
- HR directors or managers who are generalists from large enterprise organisations who want an SME experience.
- HR specialists who can make the transition to a HR generalist.

SME leaders do this consciously due to resource constraints or a lack of knowledge or belief of the importance that HR can truly contribute to an SME. The lack of visible examples of HR supporting SMEs leads to an underestimation of the value that can be created by the support of a strategic HR leader either hired or contracted.

☐ **Hygiene factors** – Salary increments, development, benefits, allowances and bonuses in many large enterprise organisations are agreed upon at the time of hiring and thereafter are a given or expectations align with past practices driving consistent policy application, e.g., x per cent annual increment or three months bonus. For SMEs, they are a constant discussion point as the very nature of these organisations leads to a context that is more fluid and dynamic than most, such as the stability of the business leads often to an inability to commit to annual salary increments, bonuses, long-term employment, career development, learning and development, finally, and sadly, even mandatory savings or severance packages are not guaranteed. At times, even labour law and health/safety regulations are managed on the cusp of being illegal.

☐ **Organisational context** – The reality hits hard very quickly for many employees who join or make a transition to SMEs, especially those previously employed by global, national, or large enterprise organisations. After a relatively short period at the company, a number of organisation factors start to raise alarm bells: dominant leadership style; lack of freedom to think and act; long decision-making times; lack of structure and process, very ad hoc working environment; misrepresented business facts; realistic growth potential; actual investment appetite; culture or way of working;

personality mismatch; and the most common, different role than what was shared at the interview. I believe everyone went into the employment relationship believing it would work out, be a great experience and they could overcome anything, however, the reality is a contrast.

- ☐ **Competitive challenges** – Given the nature of the competitive workforce landscape, especially in specific industries like IT and jobs like sales, there will always be companies, recruiters, and head-hunters tempting SME employees with the freedom to act, competitive salaries, benefits, career development opportunities and growth, and of course, the lure of significant personal financial gain if successful.

- ☐ **SME turnover** – Desired or not, can be devastating for employee productivity and morale, business momentum, continuity and sustainability, especially when the business is people reliant. It can be tragic to see the top, key talent, idea generators, or action-orientated employees resign, it can lead to a flood of other departures. The question is whether it is a 'pull' from the market forces, e.g., greater salary or development or a 'push' from the company, i.e., can't fit, can't contribute, can't grow. You have to examine what type of employees are left: are they committed shareholders, top talent, loyal or believers, underconfident or unemployable?

- ☐ **Employee communication** – More critical in an SME than I first considered as it aligns the actions of a few but critical employees, each one needs to contribute significantly. What people do each day, their time and focus will ensure no waste and higher productivity and acceleration towards organisational aspiration. With potentially fewer leaders and managers in an SME, time taken at the senior level to align and agree on the communication to the team is an investment that will pay dividends, engaging in two-way communication with the team will become a critical engagement and retention tool, the more the team feel they are on the same team and contributing the more chance to surface concerns and inputs on the way forward.

☐ **Market pay positioning** – Important matter and demands deep consideration – it is a constant dichotomy, how to deliver the business aspiration with the resources we have, constantly considering cash flow, fixed costs and employee liabilities, e.g. severance. Some founders get sucked into believing that the investor funds that they have been given, which can be in the millions, give them an endless runway of cash, however, this is rarely the case and each 'dollar' (or relevant currency) should be maximised with the goal of building a sustainable business with critical investment in critical people capability in key positions. By contrast, there are many good examples of SME leaders starting with very little and building their business without investment, following their gut feeling regarding where to invest their resources. With many different types of SME contexts, the key is to ensure that you hire the appropriate level and a number of employees at the right time; it should be a constant discussion topic. Varying your base salary and benefits positioning to ensure business aspiration delivery, e.g., if marketing is the critical success factor then investment at the 50-60th plus percentile market point may be required where support roles may deliver the required outcome with positioning at the 30-50th percentile. If you are an IT company building a disruptive new product, investing in the 75th percentile for one position may be your only chance of delivering the desired innovative product as other companies try to hire a particular scarce technology. Ongoing annual increments/increases are another challenge for SMEs.

☐ **Fixed bonuses and short- and long-term incentives** – A challenging discussion for many SMEs, with the good news being that I find most employees are realistic about any type of bonus or incentive payment as SME employees have a sense of how the company is performing. However, it can be very discouraging when an employee sees the company making a significant profit but still does not receive a payment. The details of which may vary depending on the company context, such as the founder/owner/MD/senior leaders need to reinvest the profit in order to build a sustainable business which employees will not necessarily understand unless they are clearly communicated. It is critical to find the balance between growing the business and ensuring employees understand the company's financials, recognising and rewarding employees is fundamental. In SMEs, this is no different, it may require some creative thinking and very bespoke solutions versus across-the-board approaches. As a principle, self-funding is the starting point, i.e., payments are made based on the profit made. Exceptions to this include critical skills payments (and you might call them this) to specific employees who are critical to the business and if not taken care of may be lured to another organisation by significant base salary increases.

☐ **Learning and development investment** – Another one of the most important HR discussions. Often with very little investment thinking at the early stages, SMEs run the risk of 'falling behind' or more worrying, not delivering on their aspiration because the critical capabilities, skills and knowledge are not grown or retained. SME employees also want career progression and if I had a dollar for every time a candidate told me they liked the company but needed to move to develop I would be a trillionaire! So the question becomes what is critical, who to invest in, what capabilities are critical (e.g. strategic thinking, people and financial management) and what effective, efficient and economical methods can we use to continuously develop our organisation without waste.

☐ **Performance Management** – In an SME world, PM must seem like a luxury to most, even the name sounds daunting. In its simplest form PM is the process of ensuring specific performance is being achieved. Clearly, performance is not a one-time annual event so it requires a level of evaluation depending on the criticality and relevant time frame. A simple analogy is an end-to-end manufacturing line for making chips, for example. The second is performance against targets because the process is moving fast and the risk of a particular area of the equipment malfunctioning can have huge waste/cost implications, if you don't stop the line immediately you could have thousands of wasted packets of chips. Compare this to an SME-focused on selling equipment where there is a long sales cycle, there are potentially short-term performance metrics that have been deemed necessary to achieve the sales targets, like the number of sales calls. In any context, performance evaluation and the timely resolution or feedback is critical and, most importantly, they impact the overall agreed detailed plan to achieve the business aspiration or objectives. The risk of not having timely feedback is simply that you potentially fall further behind from the expected contribution or outcome expected, an accumulation of which could be catastrophic. The key is clarity and simplicity; overwhelming leaders' time with detailed processes that either have no relevance to the overall business aspiration or are too generic to be meaningful are a waste of resources and much-needed focus time.

☐ **Recruitment and Talent** – Potentially one of the most critical accountabilities of a leader, manager and HR in an SME. It is also one of the most challenging as the talent pool is potentially very different and many SME supervisors and managers have not been trained in interview and feedback techniques, and legalities or practices, thus relying on their own given talents or techniques. Some of the horror stories I have heard about hiring in SMEs could be a book in itself. How to take a job description/profile and appropriately interview can be very daunting for many people, it really can be very nerve-racking and builds unwanted stress on some supervisors and managers. Conversely, I have seen some thrive on having the 'power' to decide someone's future, and how this manifests itself in the interview approach can be very inappropriate. When recruiting, the time, sourcing, and selection process can be very ad hoc and thus lead to a lack of talent at the right time and impact candidate confidence.

☐ **HR Investment** – Specialist HR functions demand a higher level of knowledge and, just like insurance, you never know when you need it but the consequences of not having options can lead to financial, legal and health risks. As an SME there is a resistance to spending unless it is absolutely critical. Clearly, this approach can lead to labour law legal cases, employment law compliance neglect, building negative employer branding, financial loss or employee health incidents.

☐ **Employee motivation** – Another perceived SME luxury is the lack of importance placed on recognition and employee engagement. Budgets may be significantly lower in an SME, however, the principle of developing a simple, in the moment recognition can accelerate the organisation's culture and ways of working, developing and reinforcing desired behaviours, the foundation of a successful sustainable business.

☐ **HR technology** – When you mention a human resources information system (HRIS) or other online systems and tools many SMEs quickly consider alternative low or no-cost solutions, from excel or low capability alternative solutions. The challenge is that SMEs can benefit from more sophisticated automated, low manpower-intensive systems that enable much simpler team alignment, performance awareness, and information sharing.

☐ **Scaling up** – As scaling up continues in SMEs and they move beyond their original geographical base, it may become required to move specialist talent around the world for short- or long-term assignments. Expatriate management is a very specialist area and frankly can be a very expensive investment proposition and time-consuming. The relatively low level of requirements means that SMEs and HR in particular don't have the expertise locally to know where to begin, let alone invest the required time to investigate and manage given all the other priorities in the organisation.

☐ **Location challenge** – Given the general context of SMEs, i.e., those not given significant start-up or investor funds, location is a challenge as the key is not to lock up valuable resources in investing in fixed costs that are highly expensive, especially if a large site is required. The outcome is that it may be costly and undesirable for employees to travel to certain locations outside of the public transport routes. In addition, the office will often need to be very basic at the outset, we have all heard of the home garage start-ups. Options to keep expenses low, fixed-term contract periods manageable balanced with employee wellbeing and motivation is a key consideration.

Horses for courses! Different strokes for different folks!

Throughout my SME experiences, I have seen most, if not all of the above, in some shape or form in all the companies I have supported. Adaptation of large enterprise frameworks, models, tools, and templates, supported by my ever-growing SME approaches has enabled me to achieve significant success. Let me share a few real case studies using my context, action, result (CAR) structure, to help build understanding and solidify your belief that it is possible to address most challenges with the right intervention.

Stagnant and declining revenue

Context – Growth is stagnant with declining revenue, reducing profitability, and changing customer demand.

Action – Reviews of go-to-market channels against strategic intent – develop a revised go-to-market marketing plan, developed social media capability and hired suitable talent.

Result – Return to double-digit growth through new commercial channels and customers.

Founder/owner ego impacting growth

Context – Years of leading growth-built self-belief and the challenge to accept other views and inputs to address business challenges.

Action – Two-prong approach to enable greater collaboration and collective ideation including personally coaching the leader to raise awareness of the impact, and concurrently finding suitable stakeholders to provide feedback.

Result – Collaborative sessions to drive openness and belief in others led to the development of winning business growth strategies.

Accountability conflict impacting collaboration

Context – Declining revenues lead to a finger-pointing culture and beliefs that accountability grabs would deliver improved results developed into a personal conflict which impacted collaboration and leadership alignment. Potential leadership resignation and demotivation.

Action – Constructive dialogue with key stakeholders to understand the different perspectives, from which an accountability matrix (RACI) was developed to communicate and align on the lines of responsibility.

Result – Increased accountability and clear lines of communication lead to significant improvement in business results and greater leadership focus. Retention of a key and capable leader was the primary outcome.

Start-up prioritisation anxiety

Context – Significant internal leadership anxiety over how to move forward having received funding for their two-year start-up.

Action – Leadership dialogue to gain an understanding of the business and their aspiration, development of a one-page OGSM plan, a detailed action plan developed following high impact/ high urgency exercise.

Result – Accelerated alignment of leadership and employees, performance and objective prioritisation, and dashboard development to monitor and drive continuous action plans and role definition.

Too much technical focus inhibiting business growth

Context – As is often the case, the founder/owner's background drives a high internal focus on technical/product capability.

Action – Completed strategic plan to identify critical milestones and factors to deliver the organisation's business aspiration focused on commercial, sales and marketing capabilities, and channels to market.

Result – Organisational restructure based on zero-based budgeting, commercial leadership hire, realignment of priorities and resources.

Capable people in key positions

Context – New regional MD identified a lack of leadership collaboration which was building personal conflicts and impacting business alignment.

Action – Completed two-day coaching and feedback workshops, carried out individual coaching sessions and introduced collaborative templates and tools to build collective input and depersonalisation.

Result – Improved organisational alignment, improved feedback processes to build trust, increased awareness, and reformed methods to communicate professionally through data-driven results rather than subjective personal dialogue.

Funds raised for new technology start-up

Context – After years of building the business idea and a solution blueprint, the owner/founder had to raise funds to commercialise the idea and raise funds but lacked know-how and experience.

Action – Documented a detailed business investment plan with the owner/founder and then connected with investment fund manager experts to elicit their input to strengthen the proposition.

Result – Significant initial funds raised with minimal equity given and more informed owner/founder that would strengthen ongoing fundraises.

Bringing a new idea to market

Context – Technically the idea appeared sound but untested; the funds required to build the total platform were significant and the commercialisation and go-to-market strategy not clear.

Action – Developed a roadmap to the end goal, initially identifying the market viable product (MVP) that would enable idea testing before a huge investment was required. Concurrently developed the cash flow projections required to commercialise and go to market based upon the realistic cost of acquisition (COA) metrics.

Result – Using Figma, we were able to prototype the platform for web and mobile applications to enable visualisation of the MVP and to help with tendering to gain competitive quotations.

Overseas manufacturing opportunity requires market research

Context – Specialist fibreglass technical expertise is required in an overseas market to determine market viability and project progression.

Action – Gained a strong understanding of new technology and required core capabilities to deliver on the aspiration, market research completed of broad country resources and people capabilities.

Result – Project enablers and risks identified and input into the business plan. However, this project did not go forward.

Artificial intelligence project realisation exercise

Context – Organisation attempting to enter new sophisticated customers in overseas territories with a revolutionary AI HR platform but was not making progress due to a lack of winning proposition.

Action – Developed end-to-end product demonstrations against the current context to raise awareness of the proposition to drive decision-makers' positive acceptance.

Result – Multiple discussions led to a higher level of understanding of customer pain points and the required re-work to deliver a viable investable product.

Core capabilities to drive business-impacting profitability

Context – Large food manufacturing company with successful brands challenged by financial visibility due to antiquated systems in addition to raw material direct purchasing costs limiting profit margins.

Action: Developed clarity of key capabilities required and targeted specific individual 'game changing' candidates to close the gap.

Result: Two individuals hired, created a major change in the business with the combination of world-class finance delivery coupled with innovative purchasing practices and processes which led to higher profit margins and improved cash flow/capital investment.

2

MISALIGNMENT AND ALIENATION KEY TO FAILURE

This book aims to solve a fundamental gap in the knowledge of SME HR teams in helping founders/owners/leads ensure they do not become an SME failed statistic. The supporting platform will help SME HR professionals struggling with access to expertise and resources to do their job. The use of a practical, proven toolkit and ongoing online resources will enable them to be valued in their role.

In the next chapter, we will review the bigger picture of what makes SMEs different from large enterprise organisations from a HR perspective. We will review the advantages that large enterprise organisations have and the detailed specific challenges SMEs face. Then we will start to make the transition to solutions and how to systemically overcome these challenges.

Can't see the woods through the trees!

"The task of leadership is to create an alignment of strengths so strong that it makes the system's weaknesses irrelevant."

— Peter Drucker.

In my view, the single, most consistent failure of SMEs is the lack of alignment between a senior leadership team and their employees in terms of objectives, strategies, and action plans. As an SME, there are so many priorities, nothing is perfect, and something always needs improvement. Breaking through the clutter and prioritising will ensure we do not fall into the 'can't see the woods for the trees' situation.

No capability and responsible leadership teams want this misalignment, however, when it happens, it will be highly damaging to the success of the SME delivery aspiration. It may lead to the entire team feeling a lack of sense of purpose and a shared commitment to delivery. By contrast, a highly aligned team will lead to engaged employees who are highly motivated and invested in terms of their time, talent and energy in meeting and often exceeding the aspiration of the organisation.

By the end of this chapter you will learn more about my journey, and, more importantly, how my past experiences have helped shape me as an individual and how I contributed at a significantly greater level than I ever imagined as a young man commencing his HR career.

By sharing my journey and experiences I aim to motivate, inspire, and most of all, support you as a HR professional and practitioner on your journey – whatever stage you are at. I am tired of listening to theorists alone; individuals who are great orators but have not spent a day on the front line or generally in HR positions. Each of us has the ability to contribute to improving the HR world of SMEs, however, my specific goal is to thoroughly help by providing models, tools, templates, programs and systems that are borrowed, adapted, and created specifically to help SMEs and HR teams achieve.

These experiences will provide an overview of what I have experienced in SME organisations and the impact.

No silver bullet!

I just can't imagine the complete global view of the reasons SMEs fail or, similarly, the reasons that they succeed. However, it is clear in the literature that generally speaking there is a common view that the inexperience of the owner, the lack of business/action planning, a poor idea, and funding are key reasons for failure or not maximising business opportunities. There appears to be a need to be more specific if we are to address these items. In this regard, I shared many other additional reasons above that may contribute to the failure of SMEs. Let me summarise the list that I have categorised into key themes, once again I recommend you tick those that are relevant to your context to help with personal awareness and planning:

Founder/owner
- ☐ The inexperience of the owner
- ☐ Bad idea
- ☐ Wrong motivation to start the business
- ☐ Stubborn/egotistical owner
- ☐ Leadership education, background drive agenda
- ☐ Top-down beliefs, preferences, and/or autocratic leadership style impedes creativity, innovation, and input
- ☐ Inappropriate or illegal behaviour

Clarity of direction and purpose
- ☐ Lack of roadmap, strategy, sense of purpose, and progress
- ☐ Lack of organisation clarity, roles and responsibilities
- ☐ Lack of business/action planning
- ☐ General lack of systemic prioritisation of many areas
- ☐ Market knowledge
- ☐ Capital/investment/cash flow management

Culture and ways of working

- ☐ A protective family culture that drives politics, conformity, personalisation inequity not inclusion and equity
- ☐ Contrary and/or diverse thoughts are not valued
- ☐ Lack of change and transformation culture
- ☐ Inappropriate, inconsistent, less impactful leadership style
- ☐ Lack of perceived freedom and ability to contribute

Resource constraints

- ☐ Funding
- ☐ Lack of capable people in key positions
- ☐ Investment in leadership development as they scale-up
- ☐ High pressure and stress exerted on a generally small workforce
- ☐ Cash flow management
- ☐ Investment in non-value added/lack of investment in value-added resources, tools, systems

HR factors

- ☐ Ineffective employee onboarding and cultural assimilation
- ☐ Lack of role clarity or different role than expected
- ☐ Not delivering on growth expectations or commitments
- ☐ Employment stability
- ☐ Not understand the role of HR
- ☐ Wrong HR hiring leads to wrong focus
- ☐ Lack of investment in HR leadership
- ☐ Cultural differences and fit

- ☐ Competitive forces drive turnover
- ☐ Uncompetitive compensation, benefits, and incentive policy
- ☐ Disconnected, noncritical or minimal learning and development
- ☐ Inopportune performance management
- ☐ Workforce planning and hiring practices
- ☐ Not able to invest in specialist HR support
- ☐ Employee communication and engagement
- ☐ Retention of key talent
- ☐ Lack of systems/automation, reliant on individuals
- ☐ Lack of key knowledge and capabilities, e.g., sales and marketing
- ☐ Hygiene factors such as location and working environment
- ☐ Lack of SME HR resources at an appropriate investment level

Other – what do you believe?
Add your list below:

-
-
-

There is no silver bullet to ensure SME success with so many variables at play at any one time and the emphasis of each of the above is clearly impacted by the context. The question becomes how to manage the complexity, prioritise, and get the team onboard, starting with the founder/leader. In my experience, this is often the most difficult and I have not always fully succeeded. Do you believe this list is complete? Please go online and select the areas that are impacting your business and add any others that you believe are relevant. On completion, you can see the global perception of the weighting or general view of each.

www.onehr.world

My starting belief is that two key outcomes need to be agreed upon and addressed to give the organisation its best chance of success. By viewing the above list from an outcome perspective, I believe there are two generic impacts: **misalignment and alienation**. I have associated one of these 'labels' to the list see below, however, clearly, some items can be both.

Given this belief, the formula for contributing to organisational success is:

Increase alignment, reduce alienation = effective, efficient and economical result OR put simply

↑ Alignment + Alienation ↓ = Result ↗

Cambridge Dictionary definition:

Alignment: an agreement between a group of countries, political parties, or people who want to work together because of shared interests or aims.

Alienation: to cause someone or a group of people to stop supporting and agreeing with you and/or to make someone feel that they are different and not part of a group.

Alignment needs to be emphasised as a key enabler, with alienation minimised to ensure no derailment and to drive a positive result. I believe there is an unquestionable direct correlation between the result and the emphasis placed on alignment and alienation. In my view, in any situation, even when you have to close a company, the alignment in terms of transparency with employees can drive a positive outcome if employees feel they are aware and included as part of the decision, with the potential of limiting legal consequences and more devastating, negatively impacted personal relationships. Below I have added a label for each area to provide transparency of my thoughts.

Funding	Alignment
Bad idea	Alignment
Cash flow management	Alignment
Wrong motivation to start the business	Alignment
Lack of change and transformation culture	Alignment
Lack of capable people in key positions	Alignment
General lack of systemic prioritisation of many areas	Alignment
Investment in non-value added/lack of investment in value-added resources, tools, systems	Alignment
Lack of road-map, strategy, sense of purpose, and progress	Alignment
Lack of organisation clarity, roles and responsibilities	Alignment
Lack of perceived freedom and ability to contribute	Alignment
Lack of role clarity or different role than expected	Alignment

Not delivering on growth expectations or commitments	Alignment
Not understand the role of HR	Alignment
Wrong HR hiring leads to wrong focus	Alignment
Investment in HR leadership	Alignment
Cultural differences and fit	Alignment
Compensation, benefits, recognition, and incentive policy	Alignment
Impactful learning and development	Alignment
Workforce planning and hiring practices	Alignment
Not able to invest in specialist HR support	Alignment
Retention of key talent	Alignment
Lack of systems/automation, reliant on individuals	Alignment
Lack of key knowledge and capabilities, e.g., sales and marketing	Alignment
Market knowledge	Alignment
Capital/investment/cash flow management	Alignment
Lack of SME HR resources at an appropriate investment level	Alignment
Relevant and timely performance management	Alignment
The inexperience of the owner	Alignment
Lack of business/action planning	Alignment
Stubborn/egotistical owner	Alienation
Leadership education, background drive agenda	Alienation
Top-down beliefs, preferences and/or autocratic leadership style impedes creativity, innovation, and input	Alienation

A protective family culture that drives politics, conformity, personalisation inequity not inclusion and equity	Alienation
Contrary and/or diverse thoughts are not valued	Alienation
High pressure and stress exerted on a generally small workforce	Alienation
Appropriate, consistent and impactful leadership style	Alienation
Effective employee onboarding and cultural assimilation	Alienation
Employment stability	Alienation
Competitive forces drive turnover	Alienation
Employee communication and engagement	Alienation
Hygiene factors such as location and working environment	Alienation

The first priority is to gain awareness of the current situation and context. There may be many more areas that I have not documented that are impacting the performance and results of your SME organisation. Once your context data collection has been completed, I recommend a facilitated prioritisation activity to identify those areas which are high urgency and high impact (HUHI) actions for your organisation. Given the general nature of SMEs, there are always many things to do, this makes this intervention of prioritisation key, and with the right stakeholders involved, this can accelerate the collective alignment and start to minimise alienation.

Given how long SMEs have been in existence there are significant online research papers, government studies, anecdotal statements, data points, ex-founders books, videos and of course speakers on many platforms sharing their views on the reasons for failure.

Thus I do not intend to add further links for you to review, instead, I would focus your attention on those companies that have succeeded. Again, there is significant online material for you to review. Stats are of course meaningful if they represent your context, e.g., the unfortunate truth is nine out of ten start-ups will go out of business, with only half of the remaining surviving for five years or more. Thus, a focus on sustainable organisations brings clarity and focus. Here are a few authors' thoughts:

> SMEs have a well-defined vision. Getting things done is a top priority, they master their budgets, networking is important to them, leaders keep high standards and push positivity, and they invest in the right processes and systems.
>
> — Paul Trujillo

> Successful SMEs have a good business strategy, marketing plans, strategic marketing management, satisfied employees, plan employee retention, strong management, financing, and prioritising customer service.
>
> — George N. Root III

SMEs thrive by exploiting key advantages, which we
describe as their four aces: applying technology, agility,
accelerated innovation, and attracting talent.

— John Reiners

Suffice to say, there are many documented fact-based and
anecdotal reasons and opinions for the success of an SME from
a single reason like the idea or timing or the founder's passion,
as well as multiple other reasons. Thus, I am not advocating
that a one-size-fits-all approach will drive success, however, I
have a firm belief that some fundamentals will give you the best
chance of achieving your aspiration. This can be achieved by
focusing on significant **alignment** in all areas and a reduction
of any level of **alienation** that your employees may be feeling.

It is clear that large enterprise organisations have significant
advantages in terms of leadership, strategic focus, process
orientation, cash flow and resources to mention a few. In addition,
their HR teams are often given the freedom to develop appropriate
HR strategies, policies and practices, and investment in people,
tools, and systems. However, relative to other companies in their
industry, they are on an equal footing, and it is the quality of
their leadership, business alignment and use of resources that will
define their results and ultimate success.

3

SIX FOCUS AREAS AND STEPS TO EVALUATE YOUR ORGANISATION

For SMEs, to help structure the way forward, I recommend using two separate but complementary focus areas, commencing with the organisation to guide the HR business partner and HR functional strategies and action:

I see six main areas of focus that will initially enable you to evaluate your current status and then subsequently plan your action roadmap, and just like any management system, a periodic evaluation and continuous improvement are how the most optimum outcome can be achieved.

Organisation Business Focus

Leadership alignment – There can be a tendency to share the longer-term macro business aspiration and leave it at that point, hoping the leadership team can make the appropriate assumptions, decisions and judgement to ensure delivery, e.g. grow the business to ten times the size today and sell or joint venture. Of course, this is good to know, however, in an SME thinking, too far out can distract from the immediate deliverables and the key criteria that will ensure you build a sustainable business and commercial model in the short term. The priority often has to be the execution of one customer order, the work to get to that point is key to beginning the journey. Thus taking a long term aspiration and turning it into immediate objectives and deliverables is the key, **poor planning will deliver poor performance**, this can require facilitation by HR using various tools and templates, the critical requirement is discussion, sharing and asking focused questions to ensure a strong alignment with the senior leadership team. Documenting this in a simple format that is easily understood, able to evaluate progress and direct specific action plans and continuing leadership dialogue.

Organisational alignment – Generally a leadership team will be challenged to work effectively and efficiently, and ultimately deliver the aspiration when in isolation from the entire organisation team. All levels of the team require a level of understanding of the longer-term aspiration, more importantly how they can contribute more immediately on a daily, weekly basis in terms of actions required by them. This **alignment of performance and action expectations will accelerate delivery.** Alignment also includes seeking inputs from the team on the way forward; ideas and innovations are not isolated to the senior leadership and management only. Ways of working the evolving culture are all indicators of organisational alignment and on a daily basis, the stated beliefs and visible behaviours of employees will indicate the level of understanding, motivation, and commitment. Understanding and driving appropriate beliefs can't be overstated; a key driver to daily behaviours and ultimately drives outcome or result.

Performance execution – It is often the case that successful organisations have great execution and often use this as a competitive advantage, making it a key differentiator to delivering on the organisation's aspiration. It is critical of course to have a great business plan and a winning commercial strategy and model, however, where the **rubber hits the road** is the absolute measure of achievement. In this regard, a simple but effective performance evaluation and measurement feedback process will quickly enable the identification of performance expectations that are not aligned, on, or behind the target. Discipline, timely leadership decision-making and judgements will determine the speed at which the company progresses. Execution takes incredible process discipline and has demonstrated time and time again how it can differentiate successful organisations.

Concurrent with the organisation context is the absolute need for a robust HR delivery that is focused on and complementary to the key priorities.

Human Resources Business and Functional Focus

HR business partner – In an SME, a HR leader has two critical accountabilities that are separate but intertwined. The first is a HR leader who is able to provide value to the senior leadership team, managers, and supervisors – a business partner. This person is capable of leading and facilitating cross-functional leadership teams through business sessions and is able to synthesise and collaborate at all levels of the organisation. With a deep understanding of the business via organisation alignment activity, they will need to be capable of prioritising the key focus areas and the ultimate outcome is for HR to contribute in areas that have high impact and high urgency.

HR functional partner – Concurrent with being ingrained in the business in the HRBP role, the HR leader's secondary and equally important role is to take leadership of the HR function in partnering with the business. As a starting point, a HR functional partner needs to be knowledgeable in the six core HR capabilities: performance management, recruitment, organisation development, learning, reward, and HR administration management. Other additional specialist HR areas will at some point be of value.

Disciplined HR execution – I can't emphasise enough the importance of a disciplined approach to execution in everything we do in HR, starting with supporting the business. Allocating time to your HRBP role will ensure you don't get ingrained in the easy, non-value, or non-critical activities that often are left to the HR function. The to-do lists of a HR team never end and thus the HR leader must be an action-oriented individual who has the ability to both strategise and multitask with a disciplined approach to execution. Discipline is crucial to HR competence, and when the entire team experiences your commitment to this, they will often understand your intentions. There is nothing worse than having to listen to a HRBP sharing their view on others and telling employees what they need to do and then not doing it themselves. Building belief regarding the HR function is important.

> "Discipline is the bridge between goals and accomplishment."
>
> — Jim Rohn

> "Without discipline, it is nearly impossible to be successful."
>
> — Swee Ho Tang

> "Discipline is the soul of an army. It makes small numbers formidable; procures success to the weak, and esteem to all."
>
> — George Washington

With self-discipline, most anything is possible."

— Theodore Roosevelt

It is undisputed that a significant number of SMEs fail, and it is equally undisputed that SMEs achieve success, with some going on to become large enterprises. Whatever the end-game aspiration of your SME, we believe you want to be successful in the short term. There is significant documented evidence online regarding the reasons SMEs fail, and we can therefore assume these are also the areas to focus on to be successful.

We have already discussed at length the different reasons for failure and success, which I summarised as relating to the founder/owner, clarity of direction and purpose, culture and ways of working, resources constraint, and finally, areas related to HR and hygiene factors.

Having identified the main reasons for failure, we shared a disciplined approach to address the bigger picture of driving alignment through **organisational business alignment** in terms of leadership, organisation and performance, and **HR business and functional focus** in terms of how to contribute as a HR business partner and HR functional partner, supported by a highly disciplined approach to execution.

In the next chapter, we will elaborate further on each of these six critical success factors to prevent your SME organisation from failing and becoming a statistic.

Six steps to help you be an effective SME HR practitioner: your success is our ambition!

Break out of your comfort zone and take the critical steps to become a valued (or more valued) HR leader in your SME organisation. Continuous learning and application are going to be critical to business delivery and your personal development – a win-win.

There are an estimated 200M+ SMEs in the world at this point. Whether you are a seasoned HR leader in the SME industry or just starting, I believe that everyone needs help. This help comes in different shapes and forms: 'different strokes for different HR folks'; 'horses for courses'. For most of us, living in our comfort zones is our safety blanket, even when we often want to contribute more and be more fulfilled. The risk or fear of being wrong, making a mistake, or embarrassing ourselves is more overwhelming than the perceived potential upside. I would encourage you to be brave and take these six steps to really make a difference for your company, your team, and most importantly, yourself. There really is no feeling better in the workplace than contributing.

In the following chapters, I will provide a roadmap to help guide your journey. To ensure this roadmap, support tools, and templates don't become theory only, as this book's purchaser, you will have free access (for the first year) to our global platform www.onehr.world – code SMEHR which will allow you to apply all your learnings in real-time.

This roadmap and the support tools and templates will enable you to complete a full exercise to help you assess your organisation's current status in terms of organisational alignment and your human resources business and functional focus. Post-assessment, you will be guided through the tools and templates that will support you in your journey.

HR Synergy: the sum of the whole is greater than the sum of its parts!

$$1 + 1 = 3$$

More than 20 million HR professionals working together = exponential help!

You are not alone on your journey, the power of synergy exists at the heart of www.onehr.world. Together we can truly deliver much more when we cooperate together than when we work alone. If we complement this with a can-do, results-orientated approach, providing practical models, approaches, tools, sytems, templates, and ongoing support versus rhetoric and theory, we believe you will be able to deliver meaningful HR contributions.

Your success is our aspiration!

HR is a knowledge function supported by legality, common sense, intuition, frameworks, models, processes, and constant judgements. However, to add more value you need to be constantly doing what we ask others to do – personally develop and grow! In this chapter, we will explore many of the models, tools and templates in detail which will allow you to deliver meaningful HR contributions. Imagine a world where you are equipped with appropriate knowledge to enable you to deliver, a network to ask when you are not sure and an online system of solutions to help facilitate and document your journey.

By the end of this chapter, you will be empowered to grow – we are not in the business of telling you what to do and leaving you to explore alone. Our goal is to stand alongside you, to coach, mentor, and problem-solve, build awareness and knowledge, skills, and capabilities, and ultimately support you in your role to be capable and confident. Your success is our ambition, and in this regard, we will focus on:

Self – It all starts with your acceptance that you want to grow and your motivation to continue or start the journey. We will initially help by providing a starting point through self-evaluation and reflection. Always good to start with your end in mind.

Synergy – We said you would not go on this journey alone, we and others will help you in different ways. Can you imagine a world where a community of SME HR practitioners are working in synergy, offering the power of the network that will help you develop, evolve, and deliver?

System – One of the most powerful capabilities HR practitioners can harness is knowledge management. In this regard, we will discuss the roadmap of how we will build a global SME HR system or platform (www.onehr.world) full of solutions, applications, frameworks, tools, learning materials, and templates together which will be provided free or at a very low investment and practical cost.

The key outcomes of this chapter are to provide you with a good understanding and overview of the application of the following:

- organisation business alignment assessment tool
- HR function prioritisation and focus evaluation
- gap evaluation and roadmap action building template
- core supporting models, tools and templates

I have a general belief that if you are a HR leader of an SME you would be grateful for support in various ways. My goal is to help SME HR professionals struggling with access to expertise and resources to do their job through practical and proven approaches which will enable them to excel in their job by contributing to the business and feel valued in their role. Imagine a world where you are not alone, where you are supported daily in different ways, and how much more effective you could be in your role, thereby accelerating your organisation's journey, and gaining credibility from leaders and employees, whilst developing your personal capabilities and confidence. An important point that is less spoken about but gaining attention is your personal wellbeing and mental health – a problem shared is a problem halved. My career has been a constant journey of learning, applying, and taking risks beyond my self-belief. I have had some great colleagues, mentors, trainers and friends committed to shared collective support and my personal growth specifically. I commit the same to you and totally believe that if you take the first steps to ask for help you will be surprised how impactful this can be on your life. My success can be supported by the constant business success we have had, and more importantly, the relationships I still have today with all organisations who would happily share the impact HR can have on the business with the right approach.

In this chapter we will start to unpack some of the fundamentals to help you commence the journey of *maximising alignment and minimising alienation*, ultimately helping your organisation achieve their aspiration and not become a failed statistic.

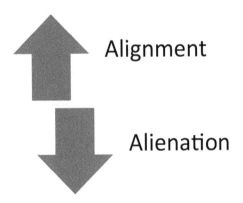

We will provide the support to help you through the process of assessment, evaluation, planning, and action management. The general starting point will include organisational business assessment, HR prioritisation evaluation, personal evaluation, HR functional evaluation, and SME HR hacks covering all priority areas of HR including organisational development, strategic

HR employee communication, performance management, learning and development, compensation management, digital HR, financial HR, and business intelligence.

Let me start by saying that our goal is not to be another source of HR superfluous HR paraphernalia, I have spent a lifetime distancing myself from survey results that are developed to drive a commercial sales agenda. Professors' theories have a value, however, given that some have not actually been employed in the HR profession, I wonder how practical and grounded their thoughts are: misinformation or non-valued added; solutions that do not work; the hype of a new model or idea that simply is not practical in the real world; exaggerated vendors whose claims are not practical; and the overpriced solutions.

Your success is our ambition, and we will always have this at the forefront of our minds. We deeply believe that your success will drive your organisation's success and ultimately help employees and economies grow.

First step roadmap… to be very clear that this is the starting point of what will be a very long (and hopefully very successful) HR OD journey.

Starting is always a challenge I find having support and a template can be a great help. A quick overview of how we will approach the kick-off of your maximising alignment and minimising alienation activities is below:

Step 1. HR self-assessment – We will start the journey focused on you, helping you raise your awareness about how I see your role and then providing you with a simple self-assessment to gauge your level of capability and preparedness seems like a great starting point. The outcome will be a very insightful assessment and the ability to develop your own action plan which will endeavour to help you with.

Step 2. Business leader (founder/owner/MD/CEO etc.) assessment – To help manage priorities and start the collaboration and alignment with your organisation's leadership team, we will provide you with a HR assessment to help understand how your most senior leader feels about the HR department's contribution to the business. In some organisations, it may be possible to combine steps 2 and 3. However, my experience is that you do not want to expose the most senior leader to this exercise in front of others if they are not totally clear themselves or can feel embarrassed. They will need their thinking time and personal alignment space first, thus, I encourage many one-on-one face-to-face meetings where you have time to ideate and facilitate the process with less risk.

Step 3. Leadership team HR assessment – To help manage priorities and start the collaboration and alignment with your organisation's leadership team (outside of your owner/founder/CEO/senior leader) we will provide you with a HR assessment to help understand how your own leadership team feel about the HR department's contribution to the business.

Step 4. HR team function maturity evaluation – Understanding your HR department's level of maturity at this time will guide your prioritisation and action planning, identifying those actions that are high urgency and high impact in support of the business aspiration.

At this point, you should have a much clearer understanding and awareness of your current pulse or status (☺☻☹) in terms of personal readiness, leadership perception, and HR functional capability. The next step is to focus on gaining an understanding of how aligned your organisation is and how knowledgeable you are as a HR business partner (HRBP).

Step 5. Business team and HR leadership alignment – A critical step that needs to be taken as soon as possible, however, at an appropriate pace, depending on your context of course. In some cases, the founder/owner and leadership may not be prepared for this level of engagement with team leaders. Once complete, it's important to align specific deliverables/objectives to the different levels of employees and the performance management process will be key, supported by strong employee communication to build understanding and engagement, and the starting point of minimising alienation.

Step 6. HR functional and employee partner (HRFP) alignment – The business aspiration is mutually exclusive (one of the issues often), however, requires a very strong alignment to all strategies, policies, processes, practises, and actions delivered by the HR functional partner, irrespective of the size of your HR team to supporting employees. This is where prioritisation due to time and financial constraints will be key, you simply can't do everything often, but you do need to drive all attention to the most important tasks like delivering the business objectives or meeting legal requirements, as well as being a strong partner to employees. This is generally through the HR functional partner activities aimed broadly at attracting, retaining, engaging, and motivating employees, and driving high levels of productivity and aligned performance.

Now you have the overall roadmap, we will go into the detailed action for each step, outlining the specific approach we are recommending. There are ten actions in total for this first part of your journey, illustrated specifically under each of the six steps below.

HR Business Partner

A1 – HR Leader Self Assessment A2 – HR Leader development plan	**Organisational Alignment**	
	A3 – Founder/ Owner/Senior Leader Alignment A4 – HR Business Alignment OGSM A5 – Senior Leadership Alignment A6 – Performance Management Alignment A7 – Models, tools and templates to support HRBP facilitation	**HR Functional Partner** A8 – HR Functional Maturity Assessment A9 – HR Functional maturity development plan A10 – HR Strategy, policy, process, practices and action planning

4

10 ACTIONS TO DRIVE SUCCESS

Step 1. Action A1 & A2 Introduction

Let's begin with you and your role...

We believe the journey begins with helping you, so we will commence by providing a very clear overview of what we believe your role requires and then give you a self-assessment tool to evaluate your current personal competency level. From here, you will be in a position to reflect on and develop a targeted growth plan that helps close the gaps towards your ambition.

Personal evaluation – self-assessment and awareness is a great starting point to ensure that you are clear on the areas you need to focus on to become highly effective in your role. As a starting point, I think it is helpful to try to articulate the general accountabilities and responsibilities of the human resources department. There are many views, particularly in the details so please bear with me as I share my thoughts, starting with a fully inclusive list not focused on SME organisations alone.

There are clearly many views on the accountabilities and deliverables of the human resources department and they are often contextual questions, e.g., if you are a small accounting firm with a total of ten employees, HR will clearly be significantly different from a global multinational entity with ten thousand employees with some core or generic requirements at a minimum. Below I will discuss what I consider to be our key accountabilities (those areas that we are accountable for) and deliverables (desired outcomes). As is my standard thought framework, I have categorised the main HR accountabilities into four boxes, the weighting and/or importance and/or relevance, which will vary depending on your context and focus of your organisation. Context includes but is not limited to your vision, business aspiration, competitive environment, geographical location, business stage, industry, type of organisation public, private, government or not-for-profit, size of organisation, beliefs and expectations of HR, and many more variables. Throughout my work I generally talk about the 'business' in this context; this refers to the organisation that you are working for, i.e., an enterprise or organisation that is engaged in professional, commercial, or industrial activities and can be for-profit or non-profit. So please don't get hung up by this term, all that is written can be applied to all organisations.

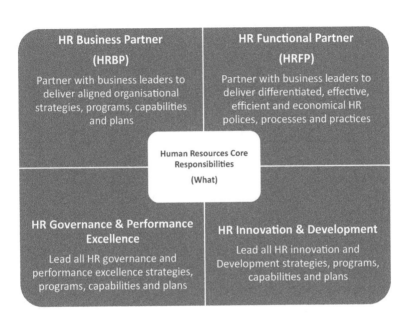

HR business partner (HRBP) – a growing and often inconsistent term and application, the human resource business partner definitions are often so broad and thus left to interpretation or misinterpretation by both senior leaders and HR professionals. The direct impact the HR function can have on the business aspiration can be significant, however, only if the scope and contribution are aligned. Yes, a HRBP is a HR professional who works directly with the senior leadership team to develop and lead a HR agenda that supports the business ambition, however, as always, the devil is in the details and a clear definition is a good starting point. Below I will share my thoughts and experiences, templates, and deliverables to illustrate. The key deliverable is the achievement of the desired performance that enables the organisation's aspirations to be achieved. This could include starting, maintaining, growing, merging, or exiting a business.

The critical key accountabilities are:

1. Business alignment – It is essential that a HRBP partner aligns with the entire organisation to build a high level of understanding and confidence about the business in detail, including aspirations, opportunities, and the journey ahead while connecting this to how business units/functions/departments, not just HR, will need to contribute/perform. This can be challenging in transformation as it can involve potential ambiguity.

2. Organisation performance – It is imperative that the HRBP partner with the leadership team to deliver a robust structure for aligning, communicating, managing, evaluating, and measuring the organisation's performance.

3. Capability development – One of the major contributions that a HRBP can make is to partner with the leadership team to identify the current, required and mature core capabilities required to deliver the organisation's ambition.

4. Organisational development – The HRBP's role in partnering with the senior leadership to move an organisation from x to y to support the business aspiration often requires agility, transformation, and/or change management leadership in many organisation development areas which may complement capability development.

5. Employer branding – Some will say that this is a HRFP area, however, I believe this to be an organisational level activity that requires partnering with senior leadership to articulate, deliver and monitor how the organisation is perceived both externally and internally. This has a major impact on many HRFP areas.

HR functional partner (HRFP) – This has always been seen as our main contribution to the delivery of business aspirations. I have given the name HR functional partner as we are often the owners of the HR functional areas, however, we must recognise that these areas also require significant collaboration and partnership with all senior, function and team leaders, and employees. We need to carefully balance our roles of leading, collaborating, facilitating, coaching, and problem-solving on a daily basis. The key deliverables are effective, efficient, and economical HR policies, processes and practices that motivate, retain, and engage high levels of organisation, team and individual productivity, and performance.

6. Performance management (PM) – A favourite subject of mine; how many PM frameworks, methods or processes are there? As HR professionals we have such a variation of thoughts, knowledge, and application with the common theme (I hope!) being the need to drive the organisational performance to meet the aspiration. What should be consistent, however often isn't, is the importance of alignment to the business plan, core values and organisational capability maturity. I often see generic forms for all levels of the organisation with historical performance indicators like punctuality, which of course has a place for some roles. I believe this is one of the single areas where HR professionals can contribute the most, yet this is often the most disconnected.

7. Talent management (TM) – Another relatively new sub-function or discipline of HR that has taken shape in the past ten plus years. Again, the application, definition, and scope of talent management vary by country and company. The term 'talent' has often meant those people who we consider 'special' – those with special or above-average abilities or skills, e.g., talent show. However, the broader definition of talent in this context means all employees are a talent. When we say all, that includes (for me!) external parties who are considered essential to the delivery of our organisation's aspirations. Some organisations consider external parties (e.g., subcontractor, outsource, remote workers) as not in scope. For me, this approach has potential implications if they are key to delivery. The traditional thinking that they are not "employees" defined as full-time permanent employees is antiquated. I remember having to tell the forty-hour-a-week outsourced staff they could not attend the annual festive party! The process breadth of TM varies; however, a good starting point is Attract – Induct – Onboard – Align – Engage – Perform – Reward – Develop – Retain. You want to bring onboard, motivate and retain the 'right' talent.

8. Recruitment Management (RM) – The definition and scope will vary, but for me, recruitment covers the buy (hire new talent), borrow and build strategies. Build is an internal process focused on developing, rewarding and engaging current employees, whereas borrowing (outsource, subcontract, contract) employees can be a very smart resourcing strategy in specific situations, however, it still demands an alignment of the job requirement and a structured approach to hiring. So let's focus on the core of recruitment for an organisation, the core sub-processes, or 4 S's as I like to refer to them: specify – a very clear description of what is required from the job; source/search – the process of finding the right candidate through the many channels open today from job boards to LinkedIn; screen – all the detailed approaches we use to screen candidates from interviewing, assessment and more recently videos; and finally, select – the process of agreeing and offering candidates.

9. Learning and development (AKA capability development or L&D – Gosh, I could write a book only about this subject, singly the potential to add the most value to an organisation and yet the most undervalued, misused, misunderstood sub-function of HR – the most undervalued area of HR that needs significant re-alignment and focus in my view. Starting with changing the title to 'capability development' with the learning and development being the 'how' we do it versus the desired outcome. The traditional L&D models are generally not working, that is assuming that they are even in a place with investment and focus is the core challenge. Every organisation requires a level of capability development, however, as long as it is seen as an expense not an investment then it will not be top of mind. L&D is a core HRFP and should be one of the the areas we partner the business with the most. This should be done almost weekly/monthly as the impact will be significant, and the L&D frameworks, delivery and desired outcomes are essential to organisational maturity. It is the most challenging area for HR professionals as we are not generally educated in this discipline, have a intrevert nature generally and for all the books written on the subject, it is not easy and demands structure and discipline to execute effectively.

10. Diversity, inclusion and equity – This has always been important and coming from a mixed English/Chinese heritage I have felt this in some way all my life. Recent tensions at a country level across the world have highlighted the power of transparency that social media and other media have provided. The topics are so varying from politics, religion, ethnicity, age, and, of course, who can forget the growing transparency of gender pay issues. In the workplace, it is critical to first identify your objectives and then align on how your organisation will lead in areas like diversity in gender, ethnicity, and disability. This will dictate how you will drive a more inclusive workplace where different cultural backgrounds (Hofsede example of collective versus individual) drive expected or normal behaviours in heterogeneous global workforces. One of the common challenges is equity in providing opportunities, managing performance and equity in reward.

11. Labour law, legal, collective bargaining, union management – Context is everything and globally there are considerable differences in terms of labour law, with a focus on being either an employer or employee-focused society. The legal frameworks vary by country, however, many have standard and generic subject topics and clauses. Finally, the presence and influence of collective bargaining agreements and (trade) unions have a rich history as countries have evolved and need to be managed accordingly.

12. Reward management – For the purposes of our discussion, reward covers the most common standard term, compensation and benefits (C&B) and a less discussed topic in some countries, i.e., recognition. I think this helps to illustrate the importance and potential impact of recognition in our reward management strategies and programs. Either a very simple or extremely complex topic depending on your country's structure, e.g., India's tax structure and multiple allowances that make up what they call TCC (total cost to company) to an SME organisation that provides base salary only, with no benefits. Sub-areas include job evaluation, market comparison, the structure of your pay bands to extremely elaborate 'buffet benefits' and total compensation packages with a pay mix that includes monthly, short-term incentive (STI) and long-term incentive (LTI) components. Overlaying these multiple organisational levels from intern to CEO, with many variations will help achieve the goal of being attractive as an employer relative to the market/ industry. Equitable and consistent application is essential, with precedent being one of the greater areas for consideration and practice versus formal policies often being discussed or litigated.

13. HR administration and employee service – At times it feels transactional and non-value added, however, the management of all the required administration and the employee service is the required foundation that illustrates an employee's value to an organisation. This starts with the onboarding process – is it heavy on non-essential paperwork or paperless? Is the service focused on the employee or the organisation's bureaucracy with non-essential activity and inconsistent delivery? I have seen horror stories where we are seen as the 'HR police' as we wield a level of authority and power over employees versus seeing them as our clients, customers, or more importantly, a critical capability and valued (human) resource.

14. Employee relations – I have separated this from the administration and delivery service as I see it as a measurable critical area in itself. The desired outcome for an organisation's leaders is to create a workplace where an employee feels that there is a positive employee/employer relationship and where positive, constructive interactions (keywords here) will drive loyal, retained, and engaged employees who believe in the organisation's core values. This of course refers to senior leadership, team leaders, supervisors, and HR, in fact, all of the organisation's formal leaders.

15. HR project management – I can't remember completing all the to-do lists I set myself in any HR role that I had because our work is never completed. The good news is that in specific areas we have HR projects, such as implementing a new HRIS or introducing a new compensation system. In these cases, there was a great sense of pride and satisfaction from moving from scoping a project through to delivery. Generally, a term used in large or enterprise companies where a HR project (defined as having a specific start and end date) is either given as additional accountability or a specific person is hired or contracted of a mix. The scope of delivery covers project objective(s), definition, resourcing, governance, evaluation, and delivery.

16. HR Systems & iOT – As HR professionals, we generally know that this accountability is very important and has the potential to significantly improve the effectiveness, efficiency and value of the HR function, however, it is complex and demands a different type of thinking, knowledge and application, whether it be the selection, development or maintenance of our HRIS,

AI/machine learning in the selection or the introduction of RPA and Chatbots to improve service delivery, it is complex and demanding. Concurrently, we need to identify and manage risk and compliance around data and employee records. At an organisational level, iOT is for most organisations an imperative that must be understood, reaching alignment of plans to support growth is not a nice to have these days.

17. Occupational, health, safety and environment – OHS&E is a term that generally applies to a specialist function that may report to HR. It really is contextual depending on the industry. Picture a steel factory – the heat, danger, and opportunities for injury versus a small insurance company. While this is quite a contrast, both require consideration of health, safety and environment, believe it or not. From a simple consideration of the way people are sitting in and on their chairs (economics) and time spent at a computer, to fully blown safety policies, systems, standards and records. You often see this on building sites, '0 safety incidents'; zero incidents are a badge of pride and reflect your organisation's consideration for the employees or contractors hired to perform. Irrespective of the industry or context, it is clear that there are current themes and evidence around wellbeing and mental health that demand a fresh review of the contribution HR has in this area. As a general rule my approach is to consider any potential HR intervention relating to health and/or wellbeing as being out of scope and requires a decision regarding what support the organisation will provide, e.g., counselling.

18. Organisation internal communication – I put this out there as a sub-function of HR as I believe it potentially has the ability to align and motivate the team significantly. Where considered and measured on its own with its own objective(s), it can be highly impactful. Whether that be an intensive partnership with the business to communicate the coming year's focus or how we communicate new ways of working, these objectives have the ability to drive beliefs and turn people on or off.

19. Expat management – In decline, but still often a necessary strategy, to grow a company. Whether hiring from outside of your country or moving an employee to another country to work, both have implications for our strategies, policies, and processes. Expat management can be a very complex area of HR as it demands 'special handling'. In my experience, one expat can be the same as managing five hundred factory employees.

20. Facilities management – One of my bugbears; it's not that it is not important, however, relative to the contribution I see HR making, this is one topic that I have been involved in, albeit reluctantly. To be clear, I do see it a little different when it comes to deciding the (re)location of the office in terms of resources available, cost, and office ergonomics – how people work together. The seating plan, for example, can drive higher levels of productivity, efficiency, and collaboration, and there are policies around computer usage and sitting guidance for optimum health and wellbeing. However, when it comes to the continued administrative task of managing the contract of a building and the teams that maintain it, including security, cleaning, and maintenance, I have a less positive view. There are many companies that specialise in this area but the challenge is that they charge a fortune, so this is often bolted onto the HR accountabilities.

> **HR governance and performance excellence (HRG&PE)** – Whilst it is critical that the HR team support the business as a priority, it is equally important that the HR function itself continuously evaluates its own performance delivery and governance in terms of external and internal compliance and adherence to planned deliverables and activities.

21. Financial management – An effective HRBP has to have a good understanding of the company's financials and must align the relevant HR strategies, policies, and budgets accordingly. It's essential to evaluate, monitor, and provide continuous feedback on performance progress and impact as appropriate, while concurrently ensuring appropriate boundaries and fiscal management, e.g., accountability boundaries around payroll.

22. Organisation HR analytics – Systematically collect, analyse and illustrate business progress against stated objectives and desired outcomes in a fact-based holistic, short, mid, and long-term view to provide the best possible base for effective management decisions through appropriate visualisation, e.g., HR dashboard.

23. HR performance metrics – Based on performance data, develop and lead activities, ensuring continued improvement of relevant aspects of HR performance: strategy, people, processes, risk (e.g., data and legal cases) and systems.

24. HR project governance – The larger the organisation, the greater the need for HR project governance, especially if the project crosses geographical, organisation, business unit or functional boundaries. We do not necessarily have to be qualified to PMP standards, however, a core understanding of how to lead a project from inception to delivery is key.

HR innovation and development (HRI&D) – Gone are the days of simply accepting the status quo. It is imperative that whatever industry you are in or your stage of business evolution – except potentially in an exit mode – that we identify opportunities to improve, evolve, transform and change the HR function delivery.

25. HR innovation and creativity – Two very different words and definitions. For me, creative is the 'tweaking' or improvement of something already existing versus innovation, which is to drive a new, potentially unheard of strategy, policy, or process, all with the goal of delivering the aspiration and/or employer differentiation.

26. HR maturity continuous improvement – Understanding your current versus the desired level of maturity in a specific area, e.g., performance management process framework can help to articulate, plan, and deliver the development required, but also set expectations.

27. Digitisation and automation – Develop and integrate updated approaches, tools and/or processes, maximising the use of digital capabilities/technologies and new media channels.

A total of twenty-six accountabilities whose value, application, and prioritisation will vary based on context.

5 Accountabilities	15 Accountabilities
HR Business Partner Partner with business leaders to deliver aligned organisational strategies, programs, capabilities and plans	**HR Functional Partner** Partner with business leaders to deliver differentiated, effective, efficient and economical HR Policies, processes and practices
3 Accountabilities	**3 Accountabilities**
HR Governance and Performance Excellence Lead all HR governance and performance excellence strategies, programs, capabilities and plans	**HR Innovation and Development** Lead all HR Innovation and Development strategies, programs, capabilities and plans

👤 HR Business Partner (5)	🏛 HR Functional Partner (15)	👍 HR Governance and Performance Excellence (3)	💡 HR Innovation and Development (3)
Business Alignment	HR Administration and Employee Service	Financial Management	HR Innovation and Creativity
Organisation Performance	Employee Relations	HR Performance Metrics	HR Maturity Continuous Improvement
Capability Development	Diversity, Inclusion and Equity	HR Project Governance	Digitisation and Automation
Organisational Development	Labour Law, Legal, Collective Bargaining, Union Management		
Employer Branding	Performance Management		
	Reward Management		
	Talent Management		
	Recruitment Management		

	Learning and Development		
	HR Project Management		
	HR Systems & IoT		
	Occupational, Health, Safety and Environment		
	Internal Communication		
	Expat Management		
	Facilities Management		

The options open to SMEs to deliver the HR accountabilities vary, I have seen five general approaches:

1. HR accountabilities are led/managed by the founder or another appointed non-HR senior leader, e.g., finance, administration and HR are combined.
2. HR is seen as a less than important function and all non-HR functional leaders are accountable for all areas related to their current team members or for external recruitment.
3. HR is seen as an administrative function, and therefore the hire of a compensation and benefits administrator is hired

with the hope they can develop or deliver the other HR functions over time as the organisation grows.

4. HR is seen as a priority and a HR manager is hired, however, the budget enables the acquisition of a functional HR manager who has only worked in another SME organisation in a similar role. Core capabilities include knowledge of local labour law, payroll, and benefits, local recruitment sourcing channels and HR administration generally the core of their capability. Often known as a HR generalist, knowledgeable in many areas but master of none and possesses very little experience and knowledge of how to partner with the business.

5. The ultimate hire is the HR leader who has made the transition to becoming a valued business partner and still possesses the HR function knowledge and practical skills to be very hands-on. Worth their weight in gold as they are a scarcity due to the perceived impact on your CV, less attractive brands, compensation and benefits package and the perceived multi-tasking and hard work required to work in HR in SMEs due to their growing and unstructured nature, with the need for creative solutions with often minimal budgets. And let's not forget patience and a level of subservience if the founder/senior leader demands the final decision in all HR-related matters and/or has limited understanding of the criticality of investment in people.

Generally speaking, I believe there are four core types of HR practitioners:

- HR generalists – Have broad knowledge and experiences of the core HR functional partner accountabilities.
- HR specialists – Have a deep knowledge of one or more of the HR functional partner accountabilities, e.g., reward (compensation & benefits), recruitment, HR administration and employee service, learning and development, HR projects, HR systems or even more specialist, e.g., strategic workforce planning and analytics or occupational, health, safety, and environment.
- Senior HR hybrid – The difference with this higher level of HR hybrid practitioner is that they would have demonstrated experience of being a HRBP in application, not in title or education only, it is a very misunderstood job title. In addition, they would be a seasoned or expert level practitioner in one plus of the main HR accountabilities.
- Junior HR hybrid – A blend of generalist/specialist, a practitioner who has either been a generalist and then moved to become a specialist or visa-versa. They have deep and broad knowledge and experience of varying HRFP, HRG&PE, or HRI&D accountabilities.

Selecting the 'right' HR Leader or using outsourced services, e.g. HRBP accountabilities, can help ensure SMEs meet the strategic and operational needs.

Step 1. Self-Awareness – A1 & A2 Action

A1. Self-assessment

Complete the self-assessment in the table below by selecting the personal maturity level that you believe you are at by circling the appropriate level or complete it online at www.onehr.world

For each of the twenty-six accountabilities you will be asked to complete what you consider to be a self-assessment of your current personal maturity level for each. In the example below, this relates to the first, which is business alignment. On completion of the self-assessment, you will be presented with a short report indicating your current level against each accountability. Once complete, you have the option to specify the job role you are either currently in or aspire to, and the assessment will then indicate your current level against the desired level, indicating your gap and development opportunities.

ACCOUNTABILITY DESCRIPTION	LEVEL
HR BUSINESS PARTNER	
Business Alignment	
I have demonstrated an exceptional understanding of the business, and facilitate and contribute at business planning sessions	5
I have a very good understanding of the business and always attend and contribute at business planning sessions	4
I have a good understanding of the business and am involved in business planning sessions when requested	3
I have a broad understanding of the business and not involved in business planning sessions	2
I lack understanding of how to contribute to business planning	1
Not part of my job accountabilities	0

Note your personal reflections below

Organisation Performance	
I have a demonstrated ability to lead the development, introduction and management of an organisation's performance framework, structure, policy, and process to drive the delivery of the business plan	5
I have supported the development, introduction, and management of an organisation performance framework, structure, policy, and process to drive the delivery of the business plan	4
I have led the management of an existing organisation performance framework, structure, policy, and process that drives the delivery of the business plan	3
I have supported the management of an existing organisation performance framework, structure, policy, and process that drive the delivery of the business plan	2
I lack understanding of how to develop an organisation performance framework, structure, policy, and process to drive the delivery of the business plan	1
Not part of my job accountabilities	0

Note your personal reflections below

Capability Development	
I have a demonstrated ability to lead the development, introduction, and management of an organisational capability plan to drive the delivery of the business plan	5
I have supported the development, introduction, and management of an organisational capability plan to drive the delivery of the business plan	4
I have led the management of an existing organisation performance framework, structure, policy, and process that drives the delivery of the business plan	3
I have supported the management of an existing organisation performance framework, structure, policy, and process that drives the delivery of the business plan	2
I lack understanding of how to develop an organisation capability plan to drive delivery of the business plan	1
Not part of my job accountabilities	0

Note your personal reflections below

Organisational Development	
I have a demonstrated ability to lead the development, introduction, and management of an organisational development plan to drive the delivery of the business plan	5
I have supported the development, introduction, and management of an organisational development plan to drive the delivery of the business plan	4
I have led the management of an existing organisation development plan that drives the delivery of the business plan	3
I have supported the management of an existing organisation development that drives the delivery of the business plan	2
I lack understanding of how I can develop an organisation development plan to drive the delivery of the business plan	1
Not part of my job accountabilities	0

Note your personal reflections below

Employer Branding	
I have a demonstrated ability to lead the development, introduction and management of an employer branding strategy and plan that is driving the delivery of the business plan	5
I have supported the development, introduction, and management of an employer branding strategy and plan that is driving the delivery of the business plan	4
I have led the management of an existing employer branding strategy and plan that is driving the delivery of the business plan	3
I have supported the management of an existing employer branding strategy and plan that is driving the delivery of the business plan	2
I lack understanding of how I can develop an employer branding strategy and plan that is driving the delivery of the business plan	1
Not part of my job accountabilities	0

Note your personal reflections below

Total HRBP Maturity Self-Assessment Rating	
Note: 20-25 High level; 15-20 Good level; 10-15 Fair level; 1-10 Low Level of HRBP maturity	

Depending on your role, your leadership team may understand the full value HR can contribute, depending on their background, thus, it would be no surprise if you had not had the opportunity to demonstrate your ability. However, I believe in HR being assertive and what they don't know they don't know so our role is to add the value and help them see it. Of course, there is the potential that you, like many, have not had the exposure or experience in the real HRBP activity and as such may lack knowledge and/or confidence. Evaluate yourself fairly and then let us help you grow.

ACCOUNTABILITY DESCRIPTION	LEVEL
HR FUNCTIONAL PARTNER	
HR Administration and Employee Service	
I have a demonstrated ability to lead the delivery of a highly effective, efficient, and economical HR administration and employee service that receives high praise and support from line management and high levels of employee satisfaction	5
I have led the delivery of a HR administration and employee service that receives minimal praise and support from line management and acceptable levels of employee satisfaction	4
I have led the delivery of a HR administration and employee service that receives no praise and support from line management and low levels of employee satisfaction	3
I have led the delivery of a HR administration and employee service that receives negative feedback from line management and low levels of employee satisfaction	2
I have led the delivery of a HR administration and employee service that requires a transformation delivery of minimal praise and support from line management and acceptable levels of employee satisfaction	1
Not part of my job accountabilities	0

Note your personal reflections below

Employee Relations	
I have demonstrated the ability to lead the delivery of a workplace where employees feel there is a very positive employee/employer relationship where constructive interaction is driving exceptional loyalty, retention, and engaged employees who believe in the organisation's core values.	5
I have led the delivery of a workplace where employees feel there is a positive employee/employer relationship where constructive interaction is driving an above-average level of loyalty, retention, and engaged employees who believe in the organisation's core values.	4
I have led the delivery of a workplace where employees feel there is an average employee/employer relationship where constructive interaction is driving an average level of loyalty, retention, and engaged employees who believe in the organisation's core values.	3
I have led the delivery of a workplace where employees feel there is a below-average employee/employer relationship where constructive interaction is driving a below-average level of loyalty, retention, and engaged employees who believe in the organisation's core values.	2
I have led the delivery of a workplace where employees feel there is a poor employee/employer relationship where constructive interaction is driving a below expectation level of loyalty, retention, and engaged employees who believe in the organisation's core values.	1
Not part of my job accountabilities	0

Note your personal reflections below

Diversity, Inclusion, and Equity	
I have a demonstrated ability to lead the delivery of a workplace where diversity in gender, ethnicity and disability is driving a highly inclusive workplace and belief is that there is a very high level of equity in providing opportunities, managing performance and reward.	5
I have demonstrated the ability to lead the delivery of a workplace where diversity in gender, ethnicity and disability is driving an above-average inclusive workplace and belief is that there is a high level of equity in providing opportunities, managing performance, and reward.	4
I have demonstrated the ability to lead the delivery of a workplace where diversity in gender, ethnicity and disability is driving an average inclusive workplace and belief is that there is an average level of equity in providing opportunities, managing performance, and reward.	3
I have led the delivery of a workplace where diversity in gender, ethnicity, and disability is driving a below-average inclusive workplace and belief is that there is a below-average level of equity in providing opportunities, managing performance and reward.	2
I have demonstrated the ability to lead the delivery of a workplace where diversity in gender, ethnicity and disability is driving a non-inclusive workplace and belief is that there is a poor level of equity in providing opportunities, managing performance, and reward.	1
I generally have no idea of the level of workplace diversity in gender, ethnicity, and disability and how this is driving an inclusive workplace and employees' beliefs regarding the level of equity in providing opportunities, managing performance, and reward.	0

Note your personal reflections below

Labour Law, Legal, Collective Bargaining, Union Management	
I have demonstrated the ability to lead the delivery of a fully compliant HR department/legal function (with all relevant labour laws and collective bargaining agreements with no outstanding claims or issues) whilst building a very positive union environment (as applicable), thereby enabling delivery of the organisation's aspiration and core values.	5
I have demonstrated the ability to lead the delivery of a partially compliant HR department/legal function (with all relevant labour laws and collective bargaining agreements with some outstanding claims or issues), whilst building a very positive union environment (as applicable), thereby enabling delivery of the organisation's aspiration and core values.	4
I have demonstrated the ability to lead a HR department/ legal function that is compliant with all relevant labour laws and collective bargaining agreements with a large number of outstanding claims or issues; we have built a positive union environment (as applicable) all of which is building a highly collaborative context, enabling delivery of the organisation's aspiration and core values.	3
I have demonstrated the ability to lead a HR department/ legal function that is compliant with all relevant labour laws and collective bargaining agreements with a large number of outstanding claims or issues; we have built a less than positive union environment (as applicable) all of which is not enabling delivery of the organisation's aspiration and core values.	2
I have not demonstrated the ability to lead a HR department/ legal function that is compliant with all relevant labour laws and collective bargaining agreements with a large number of outstanding claims or issues; we have built a negative union environment (as applicable) all of which is not supporting a highly collaborative context and delivery of the organisation's aspiration and core values.	1
Not part of my job accountabilities	0

Note your personal reflections below

Performance Management	
I have demonstrated the ability to lead the establishment of a consistent performance management delivery process that supports the agreed framework, structure, and policy that is delivering on expectations, strongly supported by line management and employees	5
I have demonstrated the ability to support the establishment of a consistent performance management delivery process that supports the agreed framework, structure, and policy that is delivering on expectations strongly supported by line management and employees	4
I have demonstrated the ability to lead the delivery of an existing performance management delivery process that supports the agreed framework, structure and policy that is delivering on expectations, strongly supported by line management and employees	3
I have demonstrated the ability to support the delivery of an existing performance management delivery process that supports the agreed framework, structure and policy that is delivering on expectations, strongly supported by line management and employees	2
I have not demonstrated the ability to lead the delivery of an existing performance management delivery process that supports the agreed framework, structure and policy that is delivering on expectations, strongly supported by line management and employees	1
Not part of my job accountabilities	0

Note your personal reflections below

Reward Management	
I have demonstrated the ability to lead the establishment of a reward strategy, policies, and processes that are delivering the strategic and operational expectations, are strongly supported by line management and are driving the desired employee beliefs and behaviour	5
I have demonstrated the ability to support the establishment of a reward strategy, policies, and processes that is delivering the strategic and operational expectations, are strongly supported by line management and are driving the desired employee beliefs and behaviour	4
I have demonstrated the ability to lead the delivery of an existing reward strategy, policies, and processes that are delivering the strategic and operational expectations, strongly supported by line management, and are driving the desired employee beliefs and behaviour	3
I have demonstrated the ability to support the delivery of an existing reward strategy, policies, and processes that are delivering the strategic and operational expectations, strongly supported by line management and are driving the desired employee beliefs and behaviour	2
I have not demonstrated the ability to lead the establishment of a reward strategy, policies, and processes that are delivering the strategic and operational expectations, are strongly supported by line management and are driving the desired employee beliefs and behaviour	1
Not part of my job accountabilities	0

Note your personal reflections below

Talent Management	
I have demonstrated the ability to lead the development, introduction and management of a Talent Management strategy and plan to drive the delivery of the business plan	5
I have demonstrated the ability to support the development, introduction, and management of a talent management strategy and plan to drive the delivery of the business plan	4
I have demonstrated the ability to lead the management of an existing Talent Management strategy, framework, structure, policy, and process that drives the delivery of the business plan	3
I have demonstrated the ability to support the management of an existing Talent Management strategy, framework, structure, policy, and process that drives the delivery of the business plan	2
I have not demonstrated the ability to develop a talent management strategy and plan to drive the delivery of the business plan	1
Not part of my job accountabilities	0

Note your personal reflections below

Recruitment Management	
I have demonstrated the ability to lead the development, introduction, and management of a recruitment management strategy and plan to drive the delivery of the business plan	5
I have demonstrated the ability to support the development, introduction, and management of a recruitment management strategy and plan to drive the delivery of the business plan	4
I have demonstrated the ability to lead the management of an existing recruitment management strategy, framework, structure, policy, and process that drives the delivery of the business plan	3
I have demonstrated the ability to support the management of an existing recruitment management strategy, framework, structure, policy, and process that drives the delivery of the business plan	2
I have not demonstrated the ability to develop a recruitment management strategy and plan to drive delivery of the business plan	1
Not part of my job accountabilities	0

Note your personal reflections below

Learning and Development	
I have demonstrated the ability to lead the development, introduction and management of a learning and development management strategy and plan to drive the delivery of the business plan	5
I have demonstrated the ability to support the development, introduction and management of a learning and development management strategy and plan to drive the delivery of the business plan	4
I have demonstrated the ability to lead the management of an existing learning and development management strategy, framework, structure, policy, and process that drives the delivery of the business plan	3
I have demonstrated the ability to support the management of an existing learning and development management strategy, framework, structure, policy, and process that drives the delivery of the business plan	2
I have not demonstrated the ability to develop a learning and development management strategy and plan to drive the delivery of the business plan	1
Not part of my job accountabilities	0

Note your personal reflections below

HR Project Management	
I have demonstrated the ability to lead the establishment of a HR ProjectRoadmap and have delivered all agreed HR Projects to the desired stated need, within the agreed timeframe and budget	5
I have demonstrated the ability to support the establishment of a HR Project Roadmap and have delivered all agreed HR Projects to the desired stated need, within the agreed timeframe and budget	4
I have demonstrated the ability to lead the management of an existing HR Project Roadmap and have delivered all agreed HR Projects to the desired stated need, within the agreed timeframe and budget	3
I have demonstrated the ability to support the management of an existing HR Project Roadmap and have delivered all agreed HR Projects to the desired stated need, within the agreed timeframe and budget	2
I have not demonstrated the ability to establish a HR Project Roadmap and have delivered all agreed HR Projects to the desired stated need, in the agreed timeframe and budget	1
Not part of my job accountabilities	0

Note your personal reflections below

HR Systems & iOT	
I have demonstrated the ability to lead the establishment of HR Systems & iOT Roadmap and have delivered all agreed HR projects to the desired stated need, in the agreed timeframe and budget	5
I have demonstrated the ability to support the establishment of HR Systems & iOT Roadmap and have delivered all agreed HR projects to the desired stated need, in the agreed timeframe and budget	4
I have demonstrated the ability to lead the management of existing HR systems & iOT Roadmap and have delivered all agreed HR projects to the desired stated need, within the agreed timeframe and budget	3
I have demonstrated the ability to support the management of existing HR systems & iOT Roadmap and have delivered all agreed HR projects to the desired stated need, within the agreed timeframe and budget	2
I have not demonstrated the ability to establish HR systems & iOT Roadmap and have delivered all agreed HR projects to the desired stated need, in the agreed timeframe and budget	1
Not part of my job accountabilities	0

Note your personal reflections below

Occupational, Health, Safety and Environment (OHS&E)	
I have demonstrated the ability to lead the development, introduction, and management of an OHS&E management strategy and plan that is driving the delivery of the business plan	5
I have demonstrated the ability to support the development, introduction, and management of an OHS&E Management strategy and plan that is driving the delivery of the business plan	4
I have demonstrated the ability to lead the management of an existing OHS&E management strategy and plan that is driving the delivery of the business plan	3
I have demonstrated the ability to support the management of an existing OHS&E management strategy and plan that is driving the delivery of the business plan	2
I have not demonstrated the ability to develop or introduce an OHS&E management strategy and plan to drive the delivery of the business plan	1
Not part of my job accountabilities	0

Note your personal reflections below

Organisation Internal Communication	
I have demonstrated the ability to lead the development, introduction, and management of an internal employee communications management strategy and plan that is driving the delivery of the business plan	5
I have demonstrated the ability to support the development, introduction, and management of an internal employee communications management strategy and plan that is driving the delivery of the business plan	4
I have demonstrated the ability to lead the management of an existing internal employee communications management strategy and plan that is driving the delivery of the business plan	3
I have demonstrated the ability to support the management of an existing internal employee communications management strategy and plan that is driving the delivery of the business plan	2
I have not demonstrated the ability to develop or introduce an internal employee communications management strategy and plan to drive the delivery of the business plan	1
Not part of my job accountabilities	0

Note your personal reflections below

Expat Management	
I have demonstrated the ability to lead the development, introduction, and management of expatriate management strategy and plan that is driving the delivery of the business plan	5
I have demonstrated the ability to support the development, introduction, and management of an expatriate management strategy and plan that is driving the delivery of the business plan	4
I have demonstrated the ability to lead the management of an existing expatriate management strategy and plan that is driving the delivery of the business plan	3
I have demonstrated the ability to support the management of an existing expatriate management strategy and plan that is driving the delivery of the business plan	2
I have not demonstrated the ability to develop or introduce an expatriate management strategy and plan to drive the delivery of the business plan	1
Not part of my job accountabilities	0

Note your personal reflections below

Facilities Management	
I have demonstrated the ability to lead the development, introduction, and management of facilities management strategy and plan that is driving the delivery of the business plan	5
I have demonstrated the ability to support the development, introduction, and management of a facilities management strategy and plan that is driving the delivery of the business plan	4
I have demonstrated the ability to lead the management of an existing facilities management strategy and plan that is driving the delivery of the business plan	3
I have demonstrated the ability to support the management of an existing facilities management strategy and plan that is driving the delivery of the business plan	2
I have not demonstrated the ability to develop or introduce a facilities management strategy and plan to drive the delivery of the business plan	1
Not part of my job accountabilities	0

Note your personal reflections below

Total HRFP Maturity Self-Assessment Rating	
Note: 20-25 High level; 15-20 Good level; 10-15 Fair level; 1-10 Low Level of HRFP maturity	

The HRFP accountabilities are the core role of most HR departments. As such, I would expect the leader to be in a good to high level of maturity depending on the role and context of course. In principle, you are the organisational expert in this area and the team will be looking to you to lead the partnership, to recommend and implement proactive strategies, interventions, solutions, and inputs using your experience and knowledge.

Once again, if you feel you lack knowledge and/or confidence after evaluating yourself fairly, let us help you contribute at a higher level.

ACCOUNTABILITY DESCRIPTION	LEVEL
HR GOVERNANCE & PERFORMANCE EXCELLENCE	
HR Financial Management	
I have demonstrated an exceptional understanding of the company's financials and have aligned the HR strategy, policy, and budget accordingly. We regularly evaluate and provide feedback on performance against agreed financial targets	5
I have demonstrated a good understanding of the company's financials and have aligned the HR strategy, policy, and budget accordingly. We evaluate and provide feedback on performance against financial targets on an ad hoc basis or when requested	4
I have demonstrated an understanding of the company's financials and have loosely aligned the HR strategy, policy, and budget accordingly. We evaluate and provide feedback on performance against financial targets when requested	3
I have demonstrated a minimal understanding of the company's financials and have not aligned the HR strategy, policy, and budget accordingly. We evaluate and provide feedback on performance against financial targets when requested	2
I have demonstrated minimal understanding of the company financials and have not aligned the HR strategy, policy, and budget accordingly. We do not evaluate and provide feedback on performance against financial targets	1
Not part of my job accountabilities	0

Note your personal reflections below

HR Performance Metrics	
I have demonstrated the ability to proactively establish a comprehensive set of HR performance metrics which have been agreed upon with the senior leadership team. These include the key HR performance KPIs relevant to the business and HR functional strategies and plans	5
I have demonstrated the ability to reactively establish a comprehensive set of HR performance metrics which have been agreed upon with the senior leadership team. These include the key HR performance KPIs relevant to the business and HR functional strategies and plans	4
I have demonstrated the ability to establish a basic set of HR performance metrics which have been agreed upon with the senior leadership team. These include the key HR Performance KPIs relevant to the business and HR Functional strategies and plans	3
I have demonstrated the ability to establish a basic set of HR performance metrics. These include the key HR performance KPIs relevant to the business and HR Functional strategies and plans	2
I have not demonstrated the ability to implement HR Performance metrics that have been agreed upon with the senior leadership team.	1
Not part of my job accountabilities	0

Note your personal reflections below

HR Project Governance	
I have demonstrated the ability to lead the development and implementation of a full HR project governance structure to support proactive continuous evaluation and leadership alignment, awareness, and action to keep on track which has been discussed and fully aligned with senior leadership.	5
I have demonstrated the ability to lead the development and implementation of a full HR project governance structure to support proactive continuous evaluation and leadership alignment, awareness, and action to keep on track which has not been discussed and fully aligned with senior leadership.	4
I have demonstrated the ability to lead the development, implementation, and management of a formal HR project governance structure autonomously through discussion and alignment with the senior leadership.	3
I have demonstrated the ability to lead the development, implementation, and management of an informal HR project governance structure autonomously without discussion and alignment with the senior leadership.	2
I have not demonstrated the ability to lead the development, implementation, and management of a HR project governance structure.	1
Not part of my job accountabilities	0

Note your personal reflections below

Total HRG&PE Maturity Self-Assessment Rating	
Note: 20-25 High level; 15-20 Good level; 10-15 Fair level; 1-10 Low Level of HRG&PE maturity	

There are going to be many factors impacting your evaluation of your HRGPE, including the level of evolution of your organisation, however, have no illusions that as busy as you may be, it is important that you have a good level of maturing in areas pertaining to HR Finances and Performance, Projects may be something that appears to be significant in nature, however, given that SMEs are new or in growth mode, there will be a need for various HR projects of varying size from selection your payroll vendor to introducing a new job description template to talent management strategies, so many opportunities to continue to evolve the HR function through incremental projects that you will need to lead, evaluation and implement.

ACCOUNTABILITY DESCRIPTION	LEVEL
HR INNOVATION AND DEVELOPMENT	
HR Innovation and Creativity	
I have significantly demonstrated the ability to lead the development and implementation of major innovative and/or creative HR solutions in alignment with senior leadership to drive business growth and delivery of the organisation's ambition	5
I have demonstrated the ability to lead the development and implementation of innovative and/or creative HR solutions in alignment with senior leadership to drive business growth and delivery of the organisation's ambition	4
I have demonstrated the ability to lead the implementation of a number of innovative and/or creative HR solutions, working autonomously	3
I have demonstrated the ability to lead the implementation of a few minor creative HR solutions, working autonomously.	2
I have not demonstrated the ability to lead the implementation of innovative and/or creative HR solutions in alignment to drive business growth and delivery of the organisation's ambition.	1
Not part of my job accountabilities	0

HR Maturity Continuous Improvement	
I have demonstrated the ability to lead the development and implementation of a HR organisational maturity development roadmap that has been agreed upon with senior leadership. A full governance structure is in place to support proactive continuous evaluation and leadership alignment, awareness, and action to keep on track.	5
I have demonstrated the ability to lead the implementation of a HR organisational maturity development roadmap that has not been agreed upon with senior leadership. An ad hoc governance structure is in place to support proactive continuous evaluation and leadership alignment, awareness, and action to keep on track.	4
I have demonstrated the ability to lead the implementation of a number of HR organisational maturity development improvements and have discussed and aligned with senior leadership. An informal HR governance structure is in place to support proactive continuous evaluation and leadership alignment, awareness, and action to keep on track.	3
I have demonstrated the ability to lead the implementation of a number of HR organisational maturity development improvements, managing these autonomously with discussion or alignment with the senior leadership.	2
I have not demonstrated the ability to lead the development and/or implementation of any HR organisational maturity development improvements.	1
Not part of my job accountabilities	0

Digitisation and Automation	
I have demonstrated the ability to lead the development and implementation of a HR digitisation and automation roadmap that has been agreed upon with senior leadership. A full governance structure is in place to support proactive continuous evaluation and leadership alignment, awareness, and action to keep on track.	5
I have demonstrated the ability to lead the development and implementation of a HR digitisation and automation roadmap that has not been agreed upon with senior leadership. An ad hoc governance structure is in place to support proactive continuous evaluation and leadership alignment, awareness, and action to keep on track.	4
I have demonstrated the ability to lead the development and implementation of HR digitisation and automation improvements. An informal governance structure is in place to support proactive continuous evaluation and leadership alignment, awareness, and action to keep on track.	3
I have demonstrated the ability to lead the development and implementation of HR digitisation and automation improvements. No governance structure is in place to support proactive continuous evaluation and leadership alignment, awareness, and action to keep on track.	2
I have demonstrated limited or no ability to lead the development and implementation of HR digitisation and automation improvements.	1
Not part of my job accountabilities	0

Total HRI&D Maturity Self-Assessment Rating	
Note: 20-25 High level; 15-20 Good level; 10-15 Fair level; 1-10 Low Level of HRI&D maturity	

It may be your belief that your SME never has a need for such HR creativity and innovation, but it is often in SMEs we have to find more for less, to deliver great value with what we have and keep fixed costs as low as possible. Given this, the HR leader has to keep themselves up to date with new ways of working and develop solutions that are of high value for employer and employee but low in capital or ongoing costs.

If you do complete the online version, you will have various ways to view your self-assessment by the four main accountabilities, individual accountability or high/low self-assessment gaps. See the sample on the following page.

A2. Personal development plan (PDP)

Complete the online PDP here www.onehr.world by identifying those areas you consider most important given your personal and business context. By completing the PDP online, we will be able to provide you with help in different ways focused on the 70/30/20 development approach.

← Self Assessment Report

HR Business Partner

HR President - Evaluation Chart ⌄
History ◀

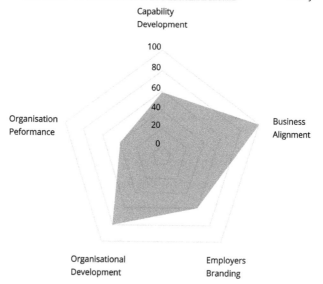

Capability
Development

100

80

60

40

20

0

Organisation
Peformance

Business
Alignment

Organisational
Development

Employers
Branding

☑ Send copy to your email

Improve

HRBP Personal Development Plan			
Current Maturity Level		Maturity Level Aspiration	
Action	SMART Goal	When	How
1.			
2.			
3.			

HRFP Personal Development Plan			
Current Maturity Level		Maturity Level Aspiration	
Action	SMART Goal	When	How
1.			
2.			
3.			

HRG&PI Personal Development Plan			
Current Maturity Level		Maturity Level Aspiration	
Action	SMART Goal	When	How
1.			
2.			
3.			

HRI&D Personal Development Plan			
Current Maturity Level		Maturity Level Aspiration	
Action	SMART Goal	When	How
1.			
2.			
3.			

Next, you can expect from this chapter a very clear path and roadmap to help you build an immediate short term, mid and long-term plan to help you to align with your SME organisation leaders. From this, you will be equipped to develop a very specific action plan that we will help you deliver in different ways.

Throughout this initial stage of your journey with us, we will provide an online space where we will provide a growing network to collaborate with, share, seek, socialise, and succeed. Because you purchased this book, you will get the first year for free. Within this platform, you will have an ear to hear you and to try to help with any questions you have. A voice in any form you want, we encourage any dialogue and sharing; we are your family and anything important to you is important to us. In addition, there is a collective system of models, tools, templates, frameworks, advice, and vendor evaluations. This is your private space, your outlet, a space to join a tribe of like-minded HR colleagues that cares about you and wants to help.

Step 2. Organisational Alignment – Action A3, A4 & A5

HR Business Partner

A1 – HR Leader Self Assessment A2 – HR Leader development plan	**Organisational Alignment**	
	A3 – Founder/Owner/Senior Leader Alignment A4 – HR Business Alignment OGSM A5 – Senior Leadership Alignment A6 – Performance Management Alignment A7 – Models, tools and templates to support HRBP facilitation	**HR Functional Partner** A8 – HR Functional Maturity Assessment A9 – HR Functional maturity development plan A10 – HR Strategy, policy, process, practices and action planning

A3. Founder/owner/most senior leader HR alignment assessment

Complete the HR alignment assessment table with your owner/founder/most senior leader online at www.onehr.world

For this important discussion, I highly recommend that you book an hour plus for a discussion, since simply sending a link might not provide the greatest clarity, however, this is an option.

For each of the twenty-six accountabilities, you will ask your most senior leader to provide an evaluation of where they believe your HR organisation is at this time on each accountability. In the example below this relates to the first, which is business alignment. On completion of the leader's assessment, you will be presented with a short report indicating the current level against each accountability as they see it.

Question to ask the business leader for each of the 26 accountabilities – what maturity level do you believe your HR organisation is at this time?

On completion you will see a space to document your discussion, for example:

```
Rating: 3
Comments:

Situation: MH
Action:
Desired Result:
```

Rating is the maturity level provided by the senior leader. Note any comments provided to guide you.

Situation – Rate urgency (low, medium or high) and impact (L M or H) and summarise your current organisational context and the relative importance of this accountability to the achievement of the organisation's business aspiration.

Action – Document any action that you have agreed or believe you need to take, once again ensuring you only document an action in the SMART format and only those that are going to have an impact versus having many non-value adding lists of things to do.

Result – What is the desired outcome from the action and how will this contribute to the achievement of the organisation's business aspiration, if it is clear that the impact is not significant I recommend you do not add.

When you commence the session with the owner/founder/ senior leader – I recommend you provide some context for the discussion and the desired outcome/objective, e.g., the purpose of this discussion is to align the HR function strategies, objectives, and priorities with yours/the organisations. There are twenty-six areas of HR, not all of them relevant for our organisation, however, by understanding and aligning your thoughts of the current maturity level of our HR function, we are then able to prioritise the HR roadmap for the coming three to twelve months which will ensure we maximise our contribution to the achievement of the organisation business aspiration. Feel free to ask as many questions as you like. Be as candid as you can so that we can ensure we are significantly aligned.

1.1 Business Alignment		
Maturity Level		**Assessment Guide**	**Evidence**
Level 5	Pro-active business partner leadership is significantly above expectation	Your HR leader/ team has demonstrated an exceptional understanding of the business and uses templates and tools to facilitate and contribute at business planning sessions	Actively and dynamically partnering in the development, alignment and delivery of organisation aspirations, strategies, and objectives, including leading/facilitating leadership, function and team sessions using appropriate transformation/change/ delivery interventions. HR functional performance significantly aligned and impacting organisation objectives delivery.
Level 4	Pro-active business partner leadership is above expectation	Your HR leader/ team has demonstrated a very good understanding of the business and always attends and sometimes contributes at business planning sessions	Actively partnering in the development, alignment and delivery of organisation aspirations, strategies, and objectives, including leading/ facilitating leadership, function and team sessions using appropriate transformation/ change/delivery interventions. HR Functional performance aligned and impacting organisation objectives delivery.
Level 3	Reactive business partner leadership, contribution meets expectation	Your HR leader/ team has demonstrated a good understanding of the business and is involved in business planning sessions when requested	As requested or assigned partnering in the development, alignment and delivery of organisation aspirations, strategies, and objectives, including leading/facilitating leadership, function and team sessions using appropriate transformation/change/ delivery interventions. HR Functional performance aligned and impacting organisation objectives delivery.

1.1 Business Alignment			
Level 2	Passive business partner leadership, contribution is below expectation	Your HR leader/team has demonstrated a broad understanding of the business and is not involved in business planning sessions	Passively partnering in the development, alignment and delivery of organisation aspirations, strategies, and objectives, including leading/facilitating leadership, function and team sessions using appropriate transformation/change/delivery interventions. HR Functional performance partially aligned and impacting organisation objectives delivery.
Level 1	No demonstrable business partner leadership	Your HR leader/team has done little or nothing to demonstrate they understand the business in detail and contribute at business planning sessions	Very passively partnering in the development, alignment and delivery of organisation aspirations, strategies, and objectives, including leading/facilitating leadership, function and team sessions using appropriate transformation/change/delivery interventions. HR Functional performance not demonstrably aligned and impacting organisation objectives delivery.
Level 0	No Idea or Not Required	HR leader/team input is not required in business planning	

Rating: Comments: Situation: Action: Desired Result:

On completion of the business leader assessment (if completed online), you will be presented with a short report providing insights into what your leader perceives of the HR function at this time. From these insights, you will once again have the ability to identify those areas that your HR teams develop to meet or exceed expectations. This alignment between business and HR leadership is an incredibly important alliance and the more aligned you are, the greater the potential partnership outcome will be.

A4. Senior Leader/HR Business Alignment

Complete the online OGSM template at www.onehr.world

Probably one of the most challenging but satisfying single-page templates that you will ever encounter. For this important discussion, I highly recommend that you complete a draft first yourself based on what you know. Then you will need to book an initial session of 1-2 hours with the most senior leader to try and complete the entire template. Generally, I have found that it takes two to four sessions before this is at a very good first draft level that they are happy to share.

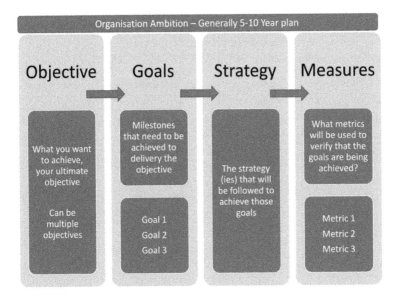

Group Vision/Target/Aim: Globally Recognised Best-In-Class One-Stop OEM Jewelry Manufacturer Financial Target/Aim: 2019 US$ 9M to 2025 - US$ 14M Revenue			
Objectives	**Goals**	**Strategies**	**Measures**
Grow? Global Brand Equity in the Silver OEM Market	- Price premium over competition from x to y - Product Design - Customer Satisfaction - Global sales revenue - Average transaction value - Customer lifetime value - Rate of sustained growth	Grow global e-commerce customers by leveraging strengths (design, product development, customer service, on-time delivery, quality, effective cost structure)	From x to y customers From x to $3M
		Grow global brand customers by leveraging strengths (design, product development, customer service, on-time delivery, quality, effective cost structure)	From x to y customers From x to $3M
		Grow global retailer customers by leveraging strengths (design, product development, customer service, on-time delivery, quality, effective cost structure)	From x to y customers From x to $3M
		Grow global other (MLM, TV Networks, Catalogues) customers by leveraging strengths (design, product development, customer service, on-time delivery, quality, effective cost structure)	From x to y customers From x to $3M

Deliver World Class Ecofriendly Manufacturing and Customer Service Excellence	- Quality - Productivity - Lead Time - Average Cost Per Item	PD - Drive MS Reputation and Customer Satisfaction by delivering exact customer requested bespoke jewelry pieces at the required specification and price by building winning **Product Development** capability	Lead from 6 week to 3-4 weeks PD with fast track for selected accounts
		PD - Drive MS Reputation and Customer Satisfaction by building winning ecofriendly and sustainable **Lean Production** capability	From 6 weeks versus market 4-5 weeks delivery time, fast track 3 weeks delivery time
		CP - Drive MS Reputation and Customer Satisfaction by delivering exceptional **Cost Price** accuracy	From 80 to 100%
		PR - Drive MS Cost competitiveness by delivering winning **Procurement and Sourcing** capability	From ? To ? Of per piece cost
		CS - Drive MS Reputation and Customer Satisfaction by delivering effective, efficient and economical world class **Customer Service** delivery	From x to y paperwork, turnaround time, accuracy

There are five key steps in this session, and we will leave the actions – the sixth step – for later in the process when you partner with department or functional leaders:

1. Document the vision and the known ambition, e.g., by 2027– often this is a ten-year horizon, achieve xxx.
2. To achieve this vision, you will need to be clear on the core (O) objectives, the 'what' you will have to achieve the vision. At this point, you have to decide whether you will focus on a ten year or shorter horizon. The key is to ensure that you have the best clarity you can have. A max of three to five core objectives is sufficient, any more and you are potentially diluting your focus and resources.
3. How will you all know when the objectives are achieved? Clear measurement is the key, what doesn't get measured will not get managed. In this case, we call them (G) goals and will complete the clarity required for performance management to be manageable. The greater transparency, visibility, and understanding.
4. For each core objective decisions need to be made around the top three to five critical (S) strategies to achieve that specific objective. These start to represent the 'how's' or path to achievement. I find the strategies to be the most challenging to articulate and facilitate, however, once completed it significantly helps the development of alignment of so many areas including organisational priorities and capability requirements.

5. Once again we need a clear understanding of how our strategic performance is tracking and the (M) measurement is the enabler. The key is to ensure you work with the leadership to document the most critical KPIs that will keep us aligned as the performance progresses. It is often easier for leaders to articulate the achievement of projects or actions than to clearly express the outcome of the strategy.

I have completed many OGSM business alignment documents and thus am very familiar with the structure, most importantly the benefits when completed appropriately and with this the challenges of doing this for your first time. I have a few tips to help ensure you are at the most strategic level as most leaders initially are too heavily focused on the how (what they need to do) versus the what (the strategic intent). I will be online to help anyone who requires support.

With the draft OGSM completed, a few iterations will ensure greater confidence and belief by all. You are ready to support your leader with the discussions with the remainder of the senior leadership team.

A5. Senior leader team/hr business alignment

Facilitate a workshop between your most senior leader and the management team as you define them, updating or making a second copy of the online OGSM template at www.onehr.world

At this point, you are probably going to be feeling like you have a very good understanding of the business from the desired outcome (vision) to the specific objectives (KPIs) that you will be using to align performance management to specific objectives and strategies that will be used to ensure we reach these KPIs. There will be much learning in this element of the template – OGSM really is a simple model and document to complete, however, it is your facilitation skills that will ensure you have a strong, compelling OGSM that clearly articulates the most senior leaders' ambition and a strategic document versus an action plan. Coaching skills can really help, it is critical to facilitate assertively, i.e., asking focused questions is a skill you will need to master. I liken it to being Sherlock Holmes arriving at a crime scene.

 Start by asking basic questions to the leadership team who you have assembled for a two to three-hour session with the senior leader in attendance, who has been requested not to comment unless you ask them to. I think the senior leader will find this quite illuminating and the insights around who knows the business will become very apparent the senior leader's communication style will always become clear.

A few helpful opening comments and questions:

The objective of this section is to help align all of us to our common desired aspiration, the outcome of which will drive our daily ambition and performance process, KPIs, and continuous feedback sessions, and of course feed into many HR organisations and people processes including capability building, hiring, performance management, and development plans as a starter. On a scale of one to five, one being not aligned at all as a leadership team and five being highly aligned all the way down to action plans, how aligned do you believe we are as a group? Document the outcome, i.e. how many ones, twos etc. OK let's commence with each of us writing down on our own pad the vision of the company including qualitative and quantitative. Facilitate the exposure of participants' responses and look for common themes and insights. On a slide have the senior leader's vision with KPIs; see how aligned they are and discuss. The next step is to outline terms of the key three to five objectives that we need to achieve to reach the vision. Again, let them work individually and then let them share and look for the similarities and differences. Next, share the senior leader's objectives. Continue the same exercise with goals, strategies, and measures.

Probably one of the most significant and satisfying feelings as a HRBP is to sit in a room of senior leaders and reflect on the completion of a business alignment or OGSM session. The sense of accomplishment is not often this high and it is just the catalyst of your HR strategic alignment.

A6. Organisational performance management

There are many approaches to managing performance within your organisation, i.e., general objective and KPI frameworks to more specific models like OKRs and MBO's PM. Irrespective of the framework you have chosen, the starting point is the core measurement of performance that will be used to align the organisation to the most important deliverables or outcomes. In this regard, the OGSM model is significantly transparent, having clearly articulated the key objective 'goals' and strategic 'measurements', and later, the key actions, which are the daily activity at the lower levels of the organisation.

Translating the OGSM (or any business plan that you use in your company) into a PM framework for your organisation is in my opinion great value as the HR function can contribute, after all it is the objectives, strategies and actions that will determine whether the ambition is achieved, assuming the OGSM clarity is appropriate.

Access the PM framework template that we have built for you at this www.onehr.world. There is a little back-office activity for you to complete to ensure clarity of which department/function will contribute to the achievement of each objective/strategy.

Depending on your organisation approach they will either be prime or shared responsibility of a particular department/ function. Once again, alignment prior to or at the beginning of the performance year will ensure greater clarity throughout the process.

At this point, we introduce 'actions' to the OGSM framework. These are the specific actions that will need to be delivered to achieve the strategies, which in turn drive the achievement of the objectives. This is where the most discipline is required as these are changing on a daily basis. The objectives and strategies are of course changing, however, the frequency will be much less on a monthly or quarterly basis. Helping build a culture of discipline around actions and monitoring delivery in real-time will ensure effective performance management and dynamic feedback and ultimately quality discussion between leaders and employees. Both qualitative and quantitative measures ensure the less tangible is still evaluated.

There is definitely a connection between the OGSM, PM, and the agreed job description or accountabilities of the department/ function and employee. It is not an exact science so doing your best is good enough.

With a clear understanding of the business and a measurement platform in place, you are well placed to move forward with taking all the inputs and aligning the HR priorities. There are so many ways to move forward and in this next section I will focus on the two that I believe are organisational and provide the best foundation for the HR priorities.

A7. Models, tools, and templates to support HRBP facilitation

At this point, I will focus on two key models and templates, many of which you will have access to through the platform at www.onehr.world. Each will provide a specific help at a particular moment or need, e.g., starting a project or HR intervention.

Business Objectives + Capability = Result

If I had my way, organisational HR leaders would be called capability directors as most of our deliverables are related to building the appropriate capability to achieve the business aspiration. With 'appropriate' being the operative word, there are simply too many capabilities to document here that deliver the desired result and indeed it is the identification, prioritisation, and development of the most important capabilities that will be the deciding factor in delivery, especially with SMEs as resources, time and funds require careful management and balance.

Using the OGSM or your own business plan approach, through facilitated discussion with leaders we extract the critical capabilities that are key to the delivery of the business aspiration. The word capabilities is often not fully understood by HR professionals, relating it to individuals rather than the organisation. Additionally, the number of capabilities is also extraordinarily long and best thought of as anything initially that will enable the delivery of the business aspirations – a few starting thoughts: customer relationship; digital marketing; leadership; organisational structure; work process; go-to marketing channels; knowledge management; organisational sustainability – there are literally thousands that can be categorised.

As the next step using the template at www.onehr.world – complete what you consider to be the core or critical capabilities and then align with your leadership team. To help facilitate the discussion, use the urgency/impact approach as it may be challenging for the leadership team to agree without such an approach. Calibrating across the leadership team is important as personal thoughts and prioritisation will drive agendas often versus organisational priorities. I generally believe that all the inputs and democracy through facilitated discussion drive the right, versus personal, outcome.

The final prioritised capabilities form the basis of organisational alignment and focus and departmental prioritisation. Essentially what we will all focus on is to continuously evaluate and measure. The driver of potentially many core HR strategies and priorities including performance management competency evaluation, hiring, and development.

For each core or critical capability, it will be necessary to ensure we have both a clear definition of what success looks like and of course current status. To help with this alignment I recommend the use of a simple maturity matrix to define, evaluate, and plan the development towards the ambition. Visit www.onehr.world for access to the organisation capability maturity matrix template.

Belief ➡ Behaviour ➡ Result

It continually surprises me that more HR professionals and practitioners are not aware of the importance and impact of the belief, behaviour, result model. It would be fair to say that beliefs are a key capability in delivering the business aspiration, others will state that this is not a capability. In summary, it does not matter, either way, it is critical that we, as organisational and HR leaders, recognise the desired beliefs versus current as these will be driving the behaviours, the tangible things employees do each day.

One of the most important moments in my HR career and an 'aha' moment that has the potential to bring greater clarity to a complex subject.

The best way to experience this live is to view at www.onehr.world, however, for the moment I ask you to imagine that your entire organisation is pervaded by many beliefs, the outcome of which is driving daily employee, team and organisational behaviour, which in turn is going to lead to a result or outcome which is either supporting or not the business aspiration. As the HR team it is critical that we focus on the beliefs that are driving the behaviour, even though the behaviours are the tangibles that we can evaluate, discuss, and provide feedback on.

The challenge is that many business leaders and HR professionals are not aware of the definition or indeed what an observation of behaviours looks like.

Exercise

I have completed this many times and I encourage you to give it a try to see the result for yourself. Select three to five leaders who have to evaluate employee performance. Stand up in front of them all and ask them to observe your behaviour for the next minute and write them down ready to share at the end. Now start raising your hands in the air like you just won a competition, then switch and put your hands down and look sad, then switch and bang the table a few times and look angry, then switch and look up like you are thinking, and then switch and smile and say stop to the group. Write their immediate responses on a board. Most replies will be that you are happy, sad, angry, thinking etc. The answer should be you put your hands in the air, you banged the table. These are the observable behaviours and facts; the rest is an assumption. Now imagine this is going on daily in organisations in PM processes in particular, many assumptions versus tangible evaluation of observable behaviours, tangible undisputed facts.

In summary, understanding what behaviour is key to understanding the organisational context and more importantly the root cause which is predominantly driven by beliefs. A practical example is when we were introducing a new route management system in Coca-Cola. We trained the drivers in the new system and were surprised when they did not follow it precisely. The drivers had their own beliefs including knowing the owner's arrival time, favourite lunch spot, route traffic. We do this often in new business interventions or processes, we focus on changing the behaviour versus spending time on the beliefs either first or concurrently.

With this behind us, let's focus on the 'beliefs' exercise – the cognitive behavioural therapy iceberg provides a nice visual to help start the dialogue and the importance of focusing on the core beliefs when developing organisational business plans.

Just like capabilities, there are many beliefs in an organisation, however, a focused targeted critical number is going to keep you on track or derail your business plan ambition.

Using the template at www.onehr.world – Complete some key beliefs that you believe are critical to the success of your business, let me start to help you with a few of the most important higher-level ones, you can think about many at all levels I believe.

Organisational – What do leaders and employees believe about the organisational ability to deliver on the business ambition, scale one to five, one being no chance, five being highly likely. Understand the gap and then qualify the numbers, what is making it a two? What is making it a four? What could make it three versus two etc.? Attempting to identify the required beliefs and behaviours to achieve the desired result will give you a strong starting point to the prioritisation of leadership and HR activity.

Functional – I am reminded of the many sales, marketing, and other functional sessions we had to discuss functional improvement ambitions and the current core beliefs. One such session was the finance team and business analysts – two groups who I believed were aligned but clearly had many different backgrounds that were impeding their ability to work together and deliver the leadership financial analysis. We used one facilitated session to identify the objective current situation, including beliefs and behaviours, and through this, we were able to bring many deep beliefs that were not enabling transparency and collaboration. Suffice to say, we opened some minds, made some tangible behavioural based action plans, followed up and delivered an excellent outcome.

Job – At the individual employee level, i.e., the coal face or where the rubber hits the road, we help to elicit simple or complex beliefs that are either going to support or hinder our progress. This can be quite an eluding activity and can give real meaning to the HR role. If employees believe that the leader is not serious about managing performance, what behaviours do we expect? If an employee believes they don't have the tools to do their job, what behaviours do we expect? If employees believe the company is setting unrealistic KPIs, what employee behaviours do we expect? Conversely, if employees believe that leaders will reward and recognise great contributions, what behaviours will we get? If employees believe that their company is contributing significantly to society, what behaviours will be expected? If candidates believe that they will get developed and expand their career opportunities by joining x organisation, what behaviour will be experienced? Too many examples but hope the positive/negative belief examples help to explain this simple yet meaningful and impactful model.

The list is endless but think about such examples in the context of the organisational culture (real versus stated); leadership style (daily versus periodically); customer focus; work processes; and ways of working.

Once you complete the first round of the most critical, you will already have a significant list to discuss with leadership and to agree on the required action if you need to change it or reinforce the action if appropriate and positive.

HR Business Partner

A1 – HR Leader Self Assessment	**Organisational Alignment**	
A2 – HR Leader development plan	A3 – Founder/ Owner/Senior Leader Alignment	**HR Functional Partner**
	A4 – HR Business Alignment OGSM	A8 – HR Functional Maturity Assessment
	A5 – Senior Leadership Alignment	A9 – HR Functional maturity development plan
	A6 – Performance Management Alignment	A10 – HR Strategy, policy, process, practices and action planning
	A7 – Models, tools and templates to support HRBP facilitation	

A8. HR functional maturity assessment

This is a topic that is close to home and one of the HR leader's key accountabilities. To ensure the HR function is delivering to the required level in appropriate areas, it is key that the HR team, starting with the HR leader, continually assess the capability of the function. To support this self-governance responsibility, I recommend a prioritisation of the required critical HR functions given the current context that you have gathered in the previous actions.

From the twenty-six HR accountabilities shared earlier, identify the top five to eight that you consider high urgency and high impact given your current strategic direction.

5 Accountabilities	15 Accountabilities
HR Business Partner Partner with business leaders to deliver aligned organisational strategies, programs, capabilities and plans	**HR Functional Partner** Partner with business leaders to deliver differentiated, effective, efficient and economical HR Policies, processes and practices
3 Accountabilities	**3 Accountabilities**
HR Governance and Performance Excellence Lead all HR governance and performance excellence strategies, programs, capabilities and plans	**HR Innovation and Development** Lead all HR Innovation and Development strategies, programs, capabilities and plans

HR Function Urgency and Impact Assessment			
HR Accountability	**Business Urgency** H M L	**Business Impact** H M L	**Select Critical 5-8**
HR Business Partner			
Business Alignment			
Organisation Performance			
Capability Development			
Organisational Development			
Employer Branding			

HR Functional Partner			
HR Administration and Employee Service			
Employee Relations			
Diversity, Inclusion and Equity			
Labour Law, Legal, Collective Bargaining, Union Management			
Performance Management			
Reward Management			
Talent Management			
Recruitment Management			
Learning and Development			
HR Project Management			
HR Systems & IoT			
Occupational, Health, Safety and Environment			
Internal Communication			
Expat Management			
Facilities Management			
HR Governance and Performance Excellence			
Financial Management			
HR Performance Metrics			
HR Project Governance			
HR Innovation and Development			
HR Innovation and Creativity			
HR Maturity Continuous Improvement			
Digitisation and Automation			

A9. HR Functional maturity development roadmap and plan

5-8 High Urgency/High Impact HR Maturity Areas			
Accountability	Current Maturity Level	Maturity Level Aspiration	SMART Goal
1.			
2.			
3.			
4.			
5.			
6.			
7.			
8.			

A10. HR Strategy, policy, process, practices, and action planning

This last action is also very critical to ensure we are partnering and delivering with the senior leadership team the best HR function strategy, policies, practices, and HR actions.

Every HR course or book will talk about the link with the organisation's aspiration, however, performing and prioritising this is the key to unlocking the true value that we can bring as one of the most important functions of any organisation.

There are many keys to unlocking the total value of the HR contribution. Each one is important, as with all judgements, the more information, insights, facts, and alignment the better the outcome I find.

There are many ways to align the HR strategy, policies, practices, and action plans with the business aspiration. I am sharing a generic model to start helping you in case (like many SMEs) you don't have a model, framework, or template. Today I met another medium organisation leader and as is very much the standard, there is no clear business plan that is shared and more importantly used to align all leaders and employees as appropriate.

OGSM link to HR strategy, policies, practices, and action plans.

Our most important contribution to the business is to partner with leaders to cascade the organisation's aspiration through effective communication and more structurally through performance management. There is and should be a domino effect from the business plan to everyday actions. Anything less and we have multiple dominoes potentially leading to a different outcome and simply a waste of what resources and time that we have.

Action 1 – take the organisation OGSM (or whatever business document you have) and complete the second level focusing on the HR contribution. Utilising the OGSM model, the strategies of the organisation OGSM become the objectives of the HR function OGSM and the organisation's measures become the goals of the HR function OGSM.

HR Function aligned to organisation OGSM

Action 2 – next step is to consider the appropriate HR strategies and measures to support the relevant objective/goal.

Action 3 – for each strategy and measure consider the actions that must be taken to support delivery. Document all the actions that you believe are critical and then carry out your prioritisation exercise using the urgency/impact matrix.

Action 4 – consider the implication of each action on current HR strategies, policies, practices, and action plans. I am confident to say that there will probably be a misalignment between your current direction and the appropriate aligned and prioritised recommendations.

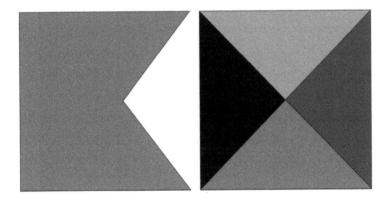

Bravo Zulu (BZ) to you – the combination of the Bravo and Zulu nautical signal flags, i.e., Bravo Zulu, also referred to as "BZ," is a naval signal, typically conveyed by flag hoist or voice radio, meaning "well done" with regard to actions, operations or performance. So, to you, I give you a huge BZ for getting this far through the book and hope that the reading and completion of some, if not all, of the supporting tools, has given you much food for thought.

It is at this point you will most definitely have both the greatest visibility of your current status of preparedness and contribution, but most importantly, your level of alignment and alienation. With such clarity comes the ability to identify the gaps that are going to drive the desired organisation's ambition and to provide a very simple but specific roadmap that will most definitely be redefined as you progress depending on your context.

I have seen different business contexts that will most certainly give you signals like a flag of where your energy and priorities are and should be, let me share a few real-life SME business examples that may guide the way that you use the insights you have gathered. These are indicative only and aim to be a few examples I have experienced that may guide your thinking. They are not exhaustive, of course, with your particular context or situation possibly being similar, completely different, or unique, we hope these examples help you and you help others by sharing your experiences through our global www.onehr.world platform built to help us excel as a HR team.

Excessive company structure – We have heard of right-sized, well, in this example, the focus is on ensuring the leadership does not walk before they can run, and does not get excited by the future when the current situation does not justify such. Specific examples include opening multiple accounting/county entities before the first revenue is achieved believing the organisation will eventually be successful in one country or market. Expanding too quickly with multiple branches, fixed cost beyond demand or capacity where often there are other options or channels to markets or manufacturing. Building internal organisation structures beyond that which is required, e.g., having multiple department heads because that is what we believe we need or have seen in the past. Cash flow is king in an SME and expending any funds in a non-value-added company or department structure is a lookout. Investment in structure has to support a sound business plan; strategy drives the structure and even though it may take longer, growing incrementally as demand is evidenced is definitely the way to progress. So, if you are sitting in an organisation that is clearly over structured or managed requires us to value each entity, department or position and the contribution they provide in the short, medium and long term. Although harder to plan, incremental managed growth correlated with revenue and/ or performance.

Unsustainable cost structure – Whether you were in the organisation from the beginning or joined partway through the journey, reviewing the cost structure is critical, especially for the fixed costs, people and infrastructure being key contributors. Having seen the benefit, I am a great believer in zero-based budgeting and the value in a SME is significant as it demands on the journey that you periodically (annually) take a step back and ask yourselves the tough questions. The principle of starting with a clean sheet and treating every shareholder/investor or revenue dollar you have as your last is a habit with adopting, we like to believe that the 'funds runway' is endless, however, the reality is that time moves quickly and without a sustainable cost structure, the pressure to perform may potentially impact smart judgments and the decision being made. Keeping costs lean whilst delivering high-value contributions and hiring capable people is a core responsibility of HR and leadership. And while not an easy one, it is worth every minute of investment in discussing this.

Service vs product vs marketing/sales vs commercial focus – Having experienced most variations, I feel this is probably one of the illuminating and interesting lookouts! Ask yourself the question: are we a service, product, marketing or commercial-focused company? Hopefully you can answer the question easily, however, then ask the question, what is the impact of this belief and/or focus? Due to the very technical nature of many entrepreneurs, there can be an excessive amount of investment of resources, time, and money on building technically wonderful products without emphasis (until it is too late) on marketing/sales and before you know it you have run out of funds. I have seen eighty to ninety per cent of the funds spent on product development with only ten to twenty left for marketing/sales, where the reality is that it should depend upon the commercial model or context be the other way around. Equally, if there's too much focus on commercials and little investment in product development we have the potential to oversell our capabilities or be replicated easily. Sustainable commercial growth is gold without a doubt and easily expressed, however, there are many variables that have to be taken into consideration, many of which are out of our control. Investment in capable people in key positions would be a priority, if the competitive difference in market will be sales of a technical product through new channels, then clearly the two first hires have to underpin this strategy.

Cost of acquisition (COA) – A term I had not heard of until I started my own SME HR solutions company. Simply and generally, every sale requires someone to buy, and the cost to acquire that buyer is the COA. A commercial, sales, or marketing term related to the cost paid to bring a potential consumer/buyer to your project, e.g., YouTube advertising videos have a cost for example US$100 per one hundred push mails, from the 105 people view and two people purchase, thus the cost of acquisition is US$50, a very high cost indeed. The reason for sharing this very important data is that a HR business partner must understand key requirements to enable a business to be successful. In the various SME experiences I have, we spent all the funds on building products versus focusing on the marketing of the products and the COA and I believe HR's role is to help priorities in all areas including cash flow management and its impact on hiring talent. If we are not clear on the COA we could be hiring people too early or building products that do not maximise the investment funds we have at our disposal.

Market viable product – Related to above and again a term learnt through facing adversity, it is also related to the HR function and the way we build HR interventions or programs. In my experience as technical professionals we try to build the ultimate product and in the process can potentially use all available resources/funds versus build sufficient products to gain revenue traction and then continue to build as funds become available. As the HR business partner, helping the leaders think through the people and fixed costs budget (runway) so that we can manage accordingly is critical, knowing the months remaining with current funds and the liabilities, e.g., severance, are key drivers of investment in product development and the product roadmap. As tough as it sounds, better to test the market and the receptiveness of the idea early than have a slow death as the realisation sinks in that fund should have been used more effectively on the journey.

Scaling up – There are a number of great books on how to scale up an organisation and it is a very important discussion to have as a leadership team (at the right time of course) and HR has a front seat in this regard with HR and people-related strategies being centre stage often. With success comes different challenges and scaling up from a small, small plus, medium, to medium-plus organisation is one of them. At the heart of scale-up is a capable and sustainable engaged and productive workforce who feel an absolute connection with the journey. Capable in the sense that it is a constant journey of balancing hiring the talent to grow the organisation with the need to keep fixed costs and associated HR accruals and the monthly run rate at an appropriate level. A daily concern is retaining key talent and knowledge management to supports business continuity, especially if you have not been able to pay at appropriate market rates. One key strategy to help is to consider building, borrowing, buying, and sadly, bouncing as required. Pivoting, being lean and agile are trending work approaches, however, in an SME it is critical to be constantly considering options that help deliver the business aspiration, there is no time for complacency or a static mentality, dynamic is the word of the day! There will be times when you have to hire externally (buy), however, using freelancers/contract employees for certain roles or contributions (borrow) is more of an option than ever with the growing number of platforms and available workforce, often looking for a second income. Accelerated promotions for internal employees can also be a great way to motivate and retain providing growth (build) opportunities and in my view loyalty to your team often reaps great rewards. Finally, it can be difficult, however, retaining people that can't add value could be detrimental to the entire organisation. As such, consider managed attrition as another tool on the journey with termination (bounce) being a realistic option if someone is unable to contribute as each salary paid has to contribute to the outcome; the decisions are more important than one considers when in motion.

None or minimal integrated performance management (PM) – A much-needed but neglected HR deliverable, the right PM approach for an SME can be challenging with the beliefs (quite rightly) that time is a challenge and outcomes a moving feast. Often the leaders of SMEs will not have experienced a working PM system/framework and those that have may have lived the 'enterprise' approach which is often elaborate and built for scale. Stepping back and identifying the objective of the PM system in your organisation is key and more importantly, building an appropriate level of investment of time. Having been employed by a number of SMEs that place little or no emphasis on PM, it was always shocking to see such waste in terms of productivity and the organisation's focus. Setting a general direction and hoping employees will know how they can maximise their contribution daily is paramount to taking what little resources you have and accepting twenty to fifty per cent waste.

Talent and capability roadmap – This is one subject I could spend a lifetime preaching about! Yes, it is complex, yes, it takes time to manage, yes, the investment of resources is one of our greatest. Having said all of that, it is, by far, often the difference between success and failure. The subject is often reflected in daily discussions or weekly KPI meetings where achievements can't be achieved due to lack of capability or people capacity, or finally seen as a key contributor to success or a reason for a failed SME. Once again, the financial resources at hand can be challenging, assuming we specify exactly what we need well but then are limited in our ability to source the 'right' person, screen and finally select and agree on a manageable package. In some industries, e.g., information technology talent is going to continue to be a huge challenge with the best talent often attracted to the high package companies who supplement this with incredible benefits. Therefore, the candidate pool, talent pipeline, workforce planning and constant need to retain employees are going to be organisational/HR imperatives demanding a HR partnership with leaders that is strategic, timely, realistic, dynamic, open and meaningful anything less will end in undesired consequences.

5

CONCLUSION

With the overwhelming priorities ever-present in an SME, it is imperative that HR partner with business leaders to help manage key imperatives using different models, tools, and templates available to us. Concurrently, ensuring the HR function itself is delivering maximum value and working on the most important contributions to help the success of the organisation.

Believing that the direction, leadership, and emotional stability of the organisation rests with the most senior leader or leadership team is the most important mistake for HR leaders. For an SME to succeed each leader and department needs to bring their 'A' game, being proactive in their contribution. In this regard, the HR department as custodians in partnering with leaders in all matters relating to people, process and capability has to contribute much more than the standard HR leader believes, a reactive, HR policy and process focus will not deliver a successful SME organisation.

In summary, for the HR department to truly contribute in an SME, their partnership with senior leadership in driving organisational alignment at all levels and reducing alienation is paramount and certainly not a nice problem to have. It is our role to ask the tough questions of everyone, to drive accountability and responsibility from all members of the team. Each contribution needs to be very specific and contribute to the whole organisation. It's true that there is generally no 'fat' in SMEs and the leaner, the more effective an organisation is, the greater the chances of success. So 'step up' HR team and 'open up' the senior leader and embrace everyone's contribution, especially the team focused on your most important asset, the enablers, the doers, the difference often between success and failure – your employees, teams and anyone external that contributes!

We have provided you with the necessary roadmap, models, tools and templates to help your organisation succeed, without a doubt the value is very contextual as some SME are incredibly well led and managed. Statistics sadly illustrate that most are not, and even those that require interventions that will help the company exceed expectations, manage resources more effectively, and lead proactively versus reactively leading the failure and closure.

HR Business Partner

A1 – HR Leader Self Assessment A2 – HR Leader development plan	**Organisational Alignment**	
	A3 – Founder/ Owner/Senior Leader Alignment A4 – HR Business Alignment OGSM A5 – Senior Leadership Alignment A6 – Performance Management Alignment A7 – Models, tools and templates to support HRBP facilitation	**HR Functional Partner** A8 – HR Functional Maturity Assessment A9 – HR Functional maturity development plan A10 – HR Strategy, policy, process, practices and action planning

There are many final thoughts I could share, the most important few are:

'Time is of the essence!'

There really is no better time to start helping your SME meet and exceed expectations for shareholders, leaders, and employees than today, evaluating the current situation and providing a very clear picture and plan for leadership to drive alignment and minimise alienation will provide an incredible starting point and foundation, no one will thank you when failure looms and you will probably be the one to execute such a terrible outcome.

'Carpe diem' (seize the day!)

I really have been there and done it, I've sat in a room and been super scared to comment, I've seen a way forward but lacked the confidence to speak up and I've dreamt of sitting with a senior leader and convincing them of how we (HR) can contribute to the business. I have been that person and today I have found a voice through facilitation. We don't need to have all the answers, we have the tools to help but we do need to find the confidence to speak up.

'Audentes fortuna iuvat' (fortune favours the brave)

I do not believe it is luck when success is achieved or when a plan comes to fruition. It is often from great thinking and planning, hard work, and a reward for those who take risks, push beyond the boundaries of the norm, rise above average execution, and truly want success and to excel. It will be a fact that if you take the next step you will grow, learn, and reinforce your personal beliefs or adapt your behaviour going forward. You will ultimately be a better HR leader, team, and business partner. Onwards and upwards my dear colleagues, you can do it and we will be standing alongside you to help you take each step forward on this journey.

Notes

Ingram Content Group UK Ltd.
Milton Keynes UK
UKHW040848280323
419292UK00004B/184